MW00659337

Bringing Sustainability to the Ground Level

Bringing Sustainability to the Ground Level

Competing Demands in the Yellowstone River Valley

Susan J. Gilbertz and Damon M. Hall

BEP
BUSINESS EXPERT PRESS
Leader in applied, concise business books

Bringing Sustainability to the Ground Level:
Competing Demands in the Yellowstone River Valley

Cover design by Divya Pidaparti, Artwork by Heins Creative Inc., Billings, MT.

Interior design by Exeter Premedia Services Private Ltd., Chennai, India

First published in 2022 by
Business Expert Press, LLC
222 East 46th Street, New York, NY 10017
www.businessexpertpress.com

ISBN-13: 978-1-63742-147-5 (paperback)
ISBN-13: 978-1-63742-148-2 (e-book)

Business Expert Press Environmental and Social Sustainability for Business Advantage Collection

Collection ISSN: 2327-333X (print)
Collection ISSN: 2327-3348 (electronic)

First edition: 2022

10 9 8 7 6 5 4 3 2 1

For Ken.

For Lindsay and Felix.

And for the people of the Yellowstone River Valley past, present, and future.

Description

Using the iconic Yellowstone River Valley of Montana as a case setting, this book is perfect for students with limited prior understanding of sustainability issues, theory, or science. The case explains how economic, environmental, and social concerns are threaded together as challenges that communities face when they imagine their long-term futures. Readers with business interests will appreciate the attention given to issues involving long-term profitability, while natural resource managers will appreciate the discussions of physical processes and nonhuman species. Others will be interested in the discussions of public policy concerns, including water law and endangered species. The case also intersects with interests of American Indians, especially concerning historical water rights. While useful and practical understandings of sustainability concepts are stressed, the details of the case expose complexities associated with improving community resilience. The authors give attention to how the valley's people express sustainability concerns, and readers are likely to recognize similar concerns in watersheds where they live. The case can, thus, function as a first step in a scaffolded curriculum designed to move students from understanding complexity into data gathering, analyses, and decision making. It provides platforms for exploring practical, theoretical, and scientific issues as linked exercises or as advanced projects. The case can also be used as a catalyst for identifying dozens of career trajectories. The National Science Foundation provided funding to pilot a similar version of this text, and the majority of the content has been empirically tested for its ability to connect STEM-based analyses to sustainability questions.

Keywords

sustainability; economic well-being; agriculture; tourism; oil and gas development; fracking; hydraulic fracturing; environmental well-being; cottonwood forests; Pallid Sturgeon; endangered species; social well-being; fairness; environmental justice; resilience; sustainable development; sustainability science; Native American; American Indian water rights; water law

Contents

Testimonials

"Gilbertz and Hall offer an engagingly written tour de force. The book is well-researched and rich in local voices. I have worked in the Yellowstone area, and studied sustainability, and came away with fresh insights about the dizzying array of issues, actors, and land uses in the watershed. They get 'place' right and avoid being parochial, by connecting local/regional phenomena to larger principles and extra-local forces."—**Richard C. Stedman, PhD, Professor and Chair, Department of Natural Resources and the Environment, Cornell University, Associate Director of the Cornell Center for Conservation Social Sciences, and Faculty Fellow at the Cornell Atkinson Center for Sustainability**

"This excellent book is an accessible and compelling way for students to understand the interconnected social, economic, and environmental dimensions of sustainability that communities are facing around the world. With descriptions of the complex practical challenges and opportunities of the Yellowstone River Valley based on hundreds of interviews with local people, Gilbertz and Hall demonstrate the legacy of environmental injustice and inequities while inspiring change through sustainability science and collective action." —**Jennie C. Stephens, PhD, Professor of Sustainability Science & Policy, Northeastern University, and author of *Diversifying Power: Why We Need Antiracist, Feminist Leadership on Climate and Energy (2020)*.**

"Finally, a comprehensive and in-depth case study that illustrates all of the threads of sustainability in a compelling context. Students will be able to grasp the interconnected complexities and challenges of sustainability because the authors weave a relevant and wellresearched narrative. This case study is an ideal teaching tool because it provides a seamless entry point to explore important concepts further and make applications to other, similar and maybe even more familiar situations."—**Jes Thompson, PhD, Professor, College of Business and Co-Director, SISU: The Innovation Institute at Northern Michigan University.**

"Sustainability of place is the most relevant and resilient approach to creating sustainable systems. Gilbertz and Hall have created a masterpiece of regional sustainable planning, beginning with the people in a place. The complexity of the Yellowstone River Valley may seem exotic, but encompasses many of the same challenges of sustainability of Southern California or the Maharashtra state of India. Competing cultural, economic, social, and environmental demands drive complex decisions that can either erode or restore ecosystems upon which all other interests depend. How we understand and navigate these differences determines the outcome.

The very personal level of engagement of the people of the Yellowstone River Valley provides the texture and tone that define the potential for common purpose. Gilbertz and Hall demonstrate that the voices of the residents in a place contain collective wisdom. Their description of water conflict very effectively framed water as the common blood of communities that defines future resiliency, and the source of blood feuds that divide communities for generations.

The challenges of conflicting cultural values emerges as the primary theme of this remarkable work by Gilbertz and Hall. Sustainability is, as they clearly define it, about how we live together now and into the future. By exploring the challenges the people of the Yellowstone River Valley face living in a place together, and identifying pathways to reconciliation, they offer real lessons for sustainability that apply to our communities as well. This book is a model for how regional sustainability planning should be approached."—**Marty D. Matlock, PhD, PE, BCEE, Professor of Ecological Engineering in the Biological and Agricultural Engineering Department at the University of Arkansas and Executive Director, University of Arkansas Resiliency Center**

Foreword

We are living in a period of extraordinary change and extraordinary challenges. To get your thinking started, consider the rate of growth of the world economy and the world population. When I was born in 1961, there were 3 billion people on Earth that relied on a global gross domestic product (GDP) of $1.4 trillion (based on current U.S. dollars). Today, in the span of less than my one human lifetime, we have reached a global population of 7.7 billion people who rely on a global GDP of $80 trillion. By 2050, that world population is expected to reach 9.8 billion (United Nations 2004) and global GDP is expected to reach $135 trillion (World Bank 2006). Let these data sink in for a minute.

What does this growth in people and the consumption associated with our GDP mean for both our lives and those of all living creatures on this finite planet? Fortunately, or unfortunately, we have some glimpses into the answer to that question. Our economy relies on fossil-fuels and the emissions from those fuels are creating changes in our global climate, which increase the frequency and intensity of wildfires, droughts, hurricanes, temperature fluctuations, sea-level rise, and more. Adding to that sobering reality, we are restricting the availability of clean water, dumping massive amounts of nitrogen and phosphorous into our land and water, warming and acidifying the world's oceans, and causing enormous numbers of species to go extinct.

At the same time, our society is becoming dangerously unequal as disparities in economic wealth and opportunity grow to epidemic levels not seen in some parts of the world since 1929, just before the start of the Great Depression. Before the COVID-19 pandemic, nearly 40 percent of Americans were unable to pay for a $400 emergency (Board of Governors 2019); 78 percent lived paycheck to paycheck (Martin 2019); 44 percent earned about $18,000 per year (Ross and Bateman 2020); and 42 percent had saved less than $10,000 for retirement (Morris 2018). In the midst of the COVID-19 pandemic, many of these people are facing real hardship and fear in an economy that unfairly distributes its benefits.

But there is reason for hope. As Charles Kettering, former head of research at General Motors, famously said, "A problem well stated is half solved." The nature of the problems we face are becoming clear and a new generation is rising to meet them. This is what Environmental Theologian Thomas Berry called *The Great Work* (2000) when he wrote, "The success or failure of any historical age is the extent to which those living at that time have fulfilled the special role that history has imposed upon them ... The nobility of our lives, however, depends upon the manner in which we come to understand and fulfill our assigned role." To my mind, the great work for today's generation lies in correcting the flaws in our political, economic, and social systems that lead to the systemic breakdowns that issues such as climate change and income inequality expose. You, the next generation of leaders, have been born into this reality and you have no choice but to respond. You did not choose this reality but you must embrace it. The nobility of your lives will be determined by how you respond to the challenges you face.

And that's where the book you are now holding comes in. It does this by shifting from "thin sustainability" to "thick sustainability," locating its analysis in a specific context—the corridor of the Yellowstone River Basin—among the actual local people who make their livelihoods and lives within this specific natural ecosystem. It presents a clear and compelling explanation of sustainability science as a critical tool for addressing the systemic challenges we face with solutions that must, by definition, also be systemic. The book points out that we can see some problems coming. For example, it is known that the regional water supply, which is vital to every aspect of life in Yellowstone River Valley, is already overallocated and there will not be enough water to satisfy all of the legitimate users. At the same time, there are increasing demands for the fossil-fuels in the Bakken field that lies under western North Dakota and northeastern Montana, and extracting those fuels requires more water. The book also points out that some problems are not yet fully known. For example, one farmer (sadly, an aging community) rightly worries that bees are disappearing as a result of chemicals that are applied on fields to boost crop yield; a tour guide worries about the future of tourism as demand rises and river access is constricted; and scientists worry about declining rainfall and snowmelt as a result of climate change. The challenge is to gather what we know and what we need to know and make our complex and highly interconnected social, economic, political, and natural systems "resilient" to avoid conflict as best as we can. This book offers the tools and models to do that in a compelling, tangible, and instructive way (such as the Yellowstone Cumulative Effects Analysis). This local specificity is so important and so needed. And unfortunately, it is not the norm.

Today, sustainability is all too often discussed in a more disconnected way, taught by a recitation of the "triple bottom line" (Elkington, 1997)—People, Planet, and Profit, or Equity, Environment, and Economy—and the Brundtland Commission (1987) definition that "Sustainable development is development that meets the needs of the present without compromising the ability of future generations to meet their own needs." We can all recite those terms such that they have become clichés. What do they really mean in practice? In many ways they are incomplete and impractical. How do we measure the 3 Ps or the 3 Es? How do we aggregate them, make trade-offs among them, come to specific policy decisions? These questions cannot be answered in the aggregate or theoretical. They must be addressed in the specific, and this book takes you there and challenges you to answer them in ways that have real import for people's lives.

I doubt that we can truly understand or achieve sustainability—or as John Ehrenfeld (2008) prefers to call it, flourishing—if we do not bring it down to this local level where real people, economies, and ecosystems reside. In the end, any implementation of efforts to address the challenges we face must be done in partnership with the people who understand, must live with and can enact those efforts. There is no other way. As our present political climate makes all too clear, the top-down imposition of solutions—whether they be fishing moratoriums, mask mandates, or pollution reductions—will be met with fierce resistance.

The antidote is careful, thoughtful, and engaged problem solving at the system level. And this book gives you the full coverage of the systemic challenges that face the precious natural and social ecosystem of the Yellowstone River that humans and nature interact in, on, and around. It tells a story—and as any science communicator will tell you "stories stick"—based on rigorous analysis. This is the best kind of science; work that is engaging, informative, educational, and pragmatic, hitting what David Stokes (1997) famously called "Pasteur's Quadrant," where "use-inspired research" breaks down the divide between basic and applied science.

It is my hope that you, the next generation of leaders, will learn from this story; consider the needs of all communities that rely on the natural world for their survival, get knee deep in the real concerns, fears, hopes, and aspirations of those communities and help us find ways to solve the problems that will continue to mount as our population, our economy, and our demands on limited resources continue to grow. No one wants to destroy the environment, the economy, or their community. As one interviewee said in this book "we just love the river so much." And more than just "love," hunting and fishing are "life enhancing" activities for many of the people who live in the Yellowstone River Basin. If we take the spirit that all want to help solve our problems but just need to be shown how, we can find a way forward. And with lesson learned, we can apply them in our own lives and community.

The future is yours to make. I challenge you to make it a future based on fairness, equality, equity, accountability, and environmental justice; one in which we all work together to create a place where everyone can thrive and flourish in a natural environment that can do the same. That is your "great work" and I encourage you to embrace it. I hope that you respond to this book's challenge with the creativity and urgency it requires. Indeed, you must, because the future of this generation and all generations to come is depending on it.

—Andrew J. Hoffman
Holcim (U.S.), Inc. Professor of Sustainable Enterprise
University of Michigan
Ann Arbor, Michigan, 2021

Preface and Acknowledgments

We launched our work in the Yellowstone River Valley in 2006 when we began the first of a series of cultural research projects there. The initial work, conducted over six months, involved interviews with over 300 people in the valley, and our goal was to have each interviewee explain why the Yellowstone River was important. On average, we spent an hour with each person, and we generated over 6,000 pages of transcribed interview data. Later, in 2012 and 2018, we conducted follow-up interviews, often with many of the same people and sometimes with newly recruited individuals.

We also helped with the Yellowstone River Basin Water Planning project sponsored by the Montana Department of Natural Resources and Conservation, 2013 to 2015. Those efforts involved meetings with hundreds of people over 18 months to determine the water management goals of the basin. We generated over 150 hours of video-recorded proceedings involving members of the public and resource specialists, such as biologists, hydrologists, and water rights administrators, to name a few.

In addition, Susan Gilbertz served for 10 years on the Technical Advisory Committee for the Yellowstone River Cumulative Effects Analysis project. That committee oversaw multiple studies examining the forms and functions of Yellowstone River, as well as the socioeconomic profiles of the people of the valley. She has also investigated the impacts of the oil and gas industry on the water resources and communities of eastern Montana.

Damon Hall was engaged in the 2006 field work as a doctoral student. His interest in data analysis and the role stakeholders can have in water resources planning and environmental policy stem from this project and continue to drive his research today. A postdoctoral research fellowship in Sustainability Science at the University of Maine revealed the power of this approach for transitioning societies toward sustainability. Since then, he has listened to the expertise of community members, then synthesized patterns of comments for decision making, and applied them to wind energy development, urban insect pollinator conservation, bicycle infrastructure planning, and community-science hydrological modeling.

Over the years, the research efforts of Gilbertz and Hall have resulted in more than 20 peer-reviewed articles reporting their findings in the valley. As presented here, this case study is based on but a few of the many intersecting economic, environmental, and social issues we have documented as important to understanding this valley, its resources, its people, and its future.

The case content includes direct quotes from the people of the valley. While the presentation maintains the confidentiality of the interviewees, we acknowledge and appreciate these inputs. Hopefully, readers will find these comments helpful as illustrations of how people grasp sustainability concepts, even when they do not talk about sustainability, per se. We appreciate the many, many people who have spoken with us over the years.

We note, with gratitude, the support received over the years from the U.S. Army Corps of Engineers, the Montana Department of Natural Resources and Conservation, and the Yellowstone River Conservation District Council. Without their support, we would never have been able to conduct the 500-plus interviews, nor would we be so familiar with the Yellowstone River Valley. We are also grateful to the National Science Foundation, which provided funding to pilot a similar version of this text in several college classrooms. In conjunction with Dr. Chris Craig, Murray State University, we can say with confidence that the majority of the content found in this case study has been empirically tested for its ability to provide a solid foundational understanding of sustainability issues and their connections to Science, Technology, Engineering and Math (STEM)-based analyses. Indeed, the idea of this case study came from Dr. Craig.

We acknowledge the local, state, and federal leadership provided during the years while the Cumulative Effects Analysis was conducted and while the State Water Plan was developed. The dedication to the Yellowstone River Valley shown by the following individuals has been profound: Greg Johnson, Eric Laux, Tiffany Vandosdall, John Kilpatrick,

Sara Meloy, Paul Azevedo, Jim Robinson, Ken Fraser, Mike Ruggles, Tony Thatcher, Don Youngbauer, Paul Gilbert, Craig Wagner, Walter Rolf, Nicole McClain, Dan Rostad, and Carol Watts.

The topics discussed in this case study are many, and any mistakes in facts or theory are ours. We were, however, able to make some important corrections based on critical feedback from the following experts, all of whom are familiar with research conducted in the Yellowstone River Valley: Warren Kellogg and Burt Williams (Cumulative Effects Analysis), Mike Backes (Pallid Sturgeon), Kathy Chase (hydrology), Chuck Dalby (hydrology and water budgets), Mark Dixon and Jonathan Friedman (cottonwood forests), Mark Elison (water rights), and Shane Doyle (American Indian rights to water in Montana). Inputs from these individuals were helpful and much appreciated.

We dedicate this case study to Warren Kellogg, Burt Williams, and Karen Boyd. Their encyclopedic and synthetic understandings of the Yellowstone River have changed the ways many people think of the valley and its future. Their influences have been forward looking and far reaching, including having formative impacts on these authors.

CHAPTER 1

Sustainability and the Yellowstone River Valley

Figure 1.1 The Yellowstone River in October, Paradise Valley

Introduction

Local tribes called it the Elk River, and when Sacajawea helped William Clark explore the Yellowstone River Valley in 1806, his journal notes regularly mention the abundant wildlife and the "handsome" islands covered with cottonwood trees. Today, one can still recognize the valley in Clark's descriptions. Wildlife, islands, and cottonwood forests are still, easily, found. Yet, the valley is not as it once was, and as we demand more from its resources, we begin to wonder if the river we know will be recognizable to future generations.

Using the iconic Yellowstone River Valley of Montana, United States, as the case setting (Figure 1.1), this book examines how the basic elements of sustainability manifest in real-life situations. The case demonstrates how economic, environmental, and social concerns are threaded together in a regional context, and it highlights the challenges that organizations, industries, and communities face when they imagine their long-term futures. The case also intersects with the interests of two of Montana's American Indian tribes—the Crow and the Northern Cheyenne peoples of southeastern Montana.

This book contains elements of widely ranging aspects of sustainability issues that different readers will find useful. Readers interested in the long-term profitability of businesses and industries will find the discussions of agriculture, tourism, and oil and gas industries of interest. Readers interested in natural resource management will appreciate the discussions of the endangered Pallid Sturgeon, cottonwood forests, and riparian areas. Other readers might be drawn to the details concerning water rights and the potential environmental justice issues that permeate management decisions involving shared resources. Regardless of your initial reasons for reading about this case, the study is designed to help you recognize the many interacting dynamics of sustainability issues.

Moreover, each of us lives in a watershed, and every community is dependent on the water resources of its region. Hopefully, the Yellowstone River Valley helps you recognize similar or parallel concerns in the watershed where you live. We encourage you to use this case study as an outline for thinking about and exploring the many regional and local sustainability issues in your backyard. This case can also serve as a platform for further exploration of multiple practical, theoretical, and scientific issues.

Sustainability's Central Question

We begin here, in Chapter 1, by discussing sustainability's central question and the traditional approaches to addressing sustainability issues. A sustainable practice is one that we know we will need to continue in the future, so we engage in our activities in ways that allow the practice to go on in perpetuity and in ways that will not jeopardize the needs of future generations (Jenkins 2016). Thus, sustainability's central question is this: Can we meet our current needs without compromising the ability of future generations to meet their needs? To answer the question, we must anticipate and understand the potential impacts of any action on our social and ecological systems. Sustainability involves maintaining and improving the healthy functioning of our human and environmental systems to enable future generations to live on this planet.

A classic example to consider toward understanding the concept of sustainability is logging. If we go into the forest and cut down all the trees, we end logging as a practice for the foreseeable future. Even if we replant seedlings, it will take many years to again have trees to harvest. Sustainable logging means harvesting a certain number of trees each year, purposefully replanting with seedlings (or ensuring sufficient seed sources from remaining trees), and allowing some trees to grow to maturity. When logging is approached in this manner, we can harvest some trees each year, and we can repeat this process indefinitely. That said, we must be careful to attend to all the factors and changes that might influence our calculations regarding how many trees to take and how many to replant each year. Factors such as adhering to legal and industry best practices to minimize effects of harvesting on soil erosion, streams, and aquatic animals must be incorporated. Knowing how to define such factors and changes is more and more difficult (Schweier et al. 2019). Also, consider how surprise factors, such as an unforeseen beetle infestation or a prolonged drought, would change our calculations. These complex interactions among human, environmental, and economic components need simultaneous consideration for societies to move toward sustainability.

As a second example at a larger scale, we can think about the world's fisheries: Are we treating fisheries in ways that will sustain fishing into the future? Or are we harvesting so many fish that many of our fisheries will collapse? And once the fisheries collapse, will they be gone forever? As noted by the United Nations, 59 percent of the world's fisheries are harvested at a maximally sustainable rate, while 35 percent of the world's fisheries are overfished and in danger of collapse (Food and Agriculture Organization of the United Nations 2020). With only 6 percent of our fisheries offering room for expanded harvests, we are seemingly on the cusp of a sustainability crisis concerning the world's fisheries. More broadly, we might think about the many other ways that wc (mis)use our oceans. Are our methods of cleaning up oil spills sufficient? Is our practice of allowing plastics to enter the oceans sustainable? Will future generations inherit oceans that are in worse condition than they are in today, or might those generations thank us for passing forward oceans that are clean and productive?

When there were not so many people on Earth, perhaps it was not so important to think about the limits of environmental resources. However, for at least 30 years, and especially now that we are approaching 10 billion people on Earth, the resources needed to sustain human life are looking scarce (Daily and Ehrlich 1992). These scarcities will, and already do, cause us to ask ourselves if we dare take everything we want and assume that the next day we can do so again. There simply may not be that many trees or fish in the world.

Underlying the central question of sustainability is an implicit charge to examine our practices willingly and critically. We need to understand if we can meet our current needs without compromising the ability of future generations to meet their needs. If our current practices will last only over our lifetime, even though we may be satisfied, we are not operating in a sustainable manner. A long-standing and key notion in sustainability is an ethical one (Shearman 1990) that assumes we understand we should leave this Earth, our planet, our home, in good condition for the next generations (Figure 1.2). As a minimal ethical requirement, we are asked to stretch our time horizon well beyond our current interests and to consider how our current practices define the future. Sustainability represents a shift in thinking from short-term gains to long-term security rooted in continuity and certainty. What will we leave for future generations? Will they continue as we have? Might we provide them with even better circumstances than were provided to us? What parts of our societies, businesses, and environments should we bolster to ensure future generations can flourish? How must we shift our thinking and behaviors?

Figure 1.2 Visitor photographing a bison near the Yellowstone River

Sustainability's Essentials: Economic, Environmental, and Social Well-Being

Traditionally, three areas of well-being, sometimes referred to as the "Three Pillars of Sustainability" (Beattie 2019; Purvis, Mao, and Robinson 2019), were identified as areas of concern to sustainability theorists, advocates, and managers. Today, we imagine the three areas as interconnected; however, much of the early work in sustainability studies tended to focus on one area or another. It is useful, still, to begin understanding sustainability by way of the traditional areas of well-being.

The first area for consideration is our economic well-being: Are the economic practices of today ones that will continue? If not, what are the changes in our practices that we should be discussing, and moving toward, so that future generations will also enjoy economic well-being? Are we creating industries and places where people want to work and live?

The second area of well-being is the environment. Here, we think about how we are using and interacting with the environment, and we ask ourselves, "Is this sustainable?" Are the ways we are using our water supplies sustainable? Are our practices regarding air quality sustainable? Are we slowly undermining ecosystems' ability to support wildlife and human life? Or are we degrading our environment and our natural resources to the point that we are leaving little or nothing for future generations? Are we simply leaving them a host of environmental messes and problems?

The third area of concern is social well-being. Here, we ask ourselves, "Are we creating, or operating within, a system that is fair to everyone?" Is it equitable? Or are we shifting some people into a class of disadvantages from which they cannot escape? Are we shifting resources in ways that the social well-being of future generations is at risk? Are our practices fair to different groups of people both in the present and in the future?

As we examine our practices and consider our alternatives, we should not expect to find simple solutions or remedies. Rather, we must be ready to meet the challenge of protecting the future. We are ready for a new generation—a generation of sustainability advocates and business leaders who are willing to think critically about our current practices and who will advocate for change (Robison 2019).

The Yellowstone River Valley: An Overview

The region selected for this case study is the Yellowstone River Valley (Figure 1.3). Approximately, half of the basin is in Wyoming, and the Yellowstone River itself begins there. Many people think of the Yellowstone River as beginning at Lake Yellowstone, in Yellowstone National Park (YNP). Indeed, from the historic Fishing Bridge in the Park, you can stand over the river as it flows out of the northern end of the lake. Technically, though, the Yellowstone River begins as merely a stream in the mountains that flank the southern end of the lake. When it exits the north end of the lake at Fishing Bridge, it is a substantial river. One wonders, how does that happen? Where does such an increase of water volume originate? Put simply, there are several sources of water coming into the lake from other streams and from some 640 thermal vents under the lake (Yellowstone National Parks Trips 2017). Thus, at the outlet from Yellowstone Lake, the Yellowstone River has much greater volume than it has entering the lake (Figure 1.4).

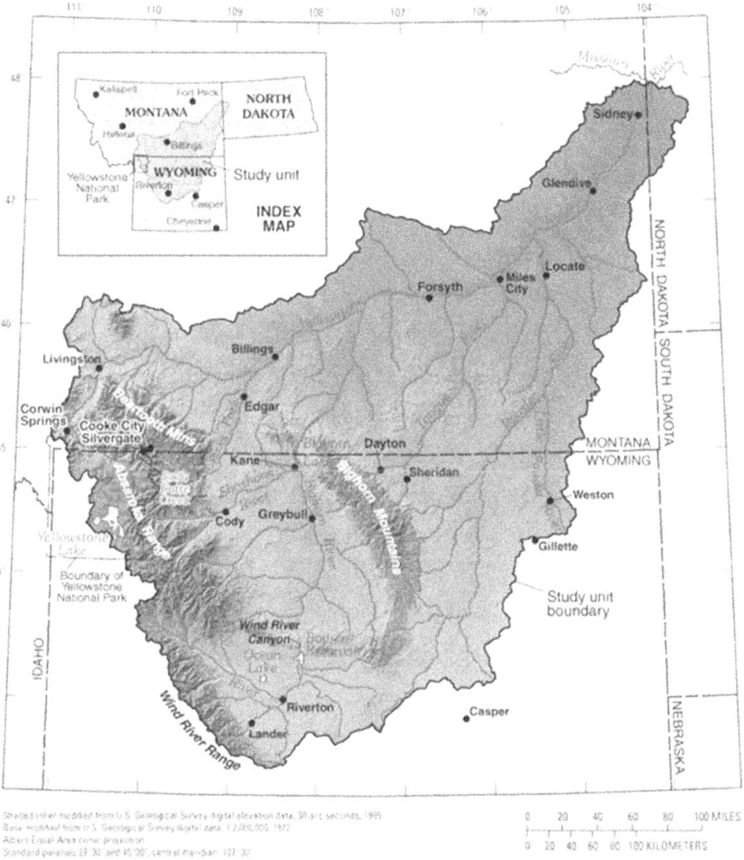

Figure 1.3 USGS map of the Yellowstone River Basin

Figure 1.4 The Yellowstone River Flowing from Yellowstone Lake in Yellowstone National Park

The Yellowstone River passes through three states, and with over 70,000 square miles (18M hectares) of land, its watershed is one of the largest drainage areas of the United States (Miller and Quinn n.d.). All the major tributaries to the Yellowstone River begin in Wyoming, and they flow north. They include the Clarks Fork of the Yellowstone River, the Bighorn River, the Tongue River, and the Powder River. For the most part, the entire drainage area flows, and the Yellowstone River flows north and east. The river flows into Montana at the northern border of Yellowstone Park at the town of Gardiner. From there, it flows over 600 river miles (965 km) across southern and eastern Montana. It continues for approximately 17 miles into North Dakota before it reaches its confluence with the Missouri River.

An interesting side note concerns the confluence in North Dakota. When Lewis and Clark came up the Missouri River in 1805, they camped at this confluence. They had to decide which of the incoming flows was a continuation of the Missouri River and which incoming flow was a tributary. Men were sent upriver, both to the northwest and to the southwest. Eventually, based on less-than-definitive reports, they decided that the branch of the river continuing to the northwest was the Missouri River. Today, we refer to this northern branch as the Upper Missouri. However, we normally consider a tributary to be a lesser river—one that *contributes* to a larger river. Interestingly, we now know that at the confluence, the two branches are essentially equal. One senior project manager with the Army Corps of Engineers (COE) explained that, "if we were to choose the continuation of the Missouri River, today, it would be a coin toss" (Greg Johnson, personal communication, July 02, 2020). In other words, we might rightly refer to the southern branch—the river we call the Yellowstone—as the Missouri River.

Our case study begins at the border town of Gardiner, Montana. Inside YNP, the river is managed by park officials, and decisions are in accordance with park purposes and values. The river is managed very differently once it comes out of the park and begins to intersect with private property. Indeed, beyond the park boundaries, over 80 percent of the riverbank is privately owned (U.S. Army Corps of Engineers and Yellowstone River Conservation District Council 2015, 4). We will look closely at what happens to the river outside the park where federal, state, and local authorities attempt to balance managing the public resources of the river with lawful private interests.

Also, much of this case study will focus on the practices of the people living near the river, or what is referred to as the main stem corridor of the river. It is in this area where most of the people live, where the most profitable economic activities occur, where environmental resources are most extensively used, and where some of the most complex social dynamics exist.

This case study examines the activities of the people and communities along the river corridor itself. Across 11 counties in Montana and one in North Dakota, the primary towns discussed in this case study include Gardiner, Livingston, Billings, Forsyth, Miles City, Glendive, and Sidney. Many of the other towns and communities along the river are strikingly small, with populations of only a few hundred people. Some of the smaller communities have only a few streets, or even just one paved (or sometimes unpaved) main street. Of course, other people live in the valley; however, those numbers are small and add only a few thousand to the total populations of each county. Unsurprisingly, many of the people living in this region embrace rural identities, and the region is generally characterized by rural activities. The largest city in Montana is Billings, with more than 100,000 people, and it is the only example of a rural/urban interface in the valley (U.S. Census Bureau 2019b).

Each of these towns and communities depends on the Yellowstone River for their physical and economic well-being. For instance, they all get their drinking water out of the river or from wells that are dependent on subsurface river flows. They also, eventually, allow much of their treated wastewater to reenter the river, often quite directly. That means the farther downstream a person is, the more times their water has recycled through different towns and different systems of drinking water and wastewater treatment. Even in Billings, approximately mid-point along the length of the river, the water has already been used several times. The river is also important to these communities because of the agricultural activities that are supported via irrigation projects and systems. In turn, and especially in the small towns, the economies of those communities are dependent on agricultural families for their economic well-being. It is important to keep in mind that for many of these communities, their economies are primarily defined in terms of agricultural activities.

Yellowstone River Cumulative Effects Analysis

After extensive flooding in 1996 and 1997, dozens of studies examined the mechanics, biologic communities, and uses of the Yellowstone River. As sets of resources, these studies contributed to the Yellowstone River Cumulative Effects Analysis (CEA), an in-depth, multidisciplinary look at the responses of the river to incremental human activities over the course of time, published in 2015 (YRCDC). Many of the details presented throughout this case study draw from the extensive resources associated with the CEA. As a reader, you may want to access those studies directly, which you can do by visiting the Yellowstone River Clearinghouse (n.d.), maintained by the Montana State Library.

The clearinghouse also hosts an interactive map that makes it convenient for readers to look at various elements of the case study in close detail (Yellowstone River Conservation Districts Council n.d.b.). We encourage you to look at the historic and contemporary images housed there. Before your first visit to the map, it will be helpful if you know to approach your viewing in terms of the terminology of the CEA study designers who examined the river as a series of reaches. Each river reach is characterized and defined by physiographic elements—a definable set of physical attributes that shape the river for a determined distance. When the characteristics of the river change, a new reach is designated. Some reaches are rather short, and others are much longer, with differences in length being determined by changes in attributes, including sediment types, sedimentation, channel sinuosity, and so on. For instance, Reach A16 is defined by much meandering among several channels of the river. In comparison, Reach PC19 is in one main channel, with virtually no side channels or sandbars. In the interactive map, you will be able to zoom in on images that will make it easier to understand the content of this case study. While this case study is complete without the interactive map, we think it will be far more interesting for readers who periodically look at the electronic images.

Preview of the Chapters

In Chapter 2, we will examine three key economic activities in the valley: agriculture, tourism, and oil and gas development. We address agriculture as our first area of discussion because farming and ranching are the dominant activities throughout much of the valley. Second, we will examine tourism. There are tourism activities throughout the valley, but for our purposes we will narrow our focus to the tourism generated near the entrance to YNP, specifically in the Livingston and Gardiner areas. Finally, we will turn to oil and gas development. When one considers the economy of the lower reaches of the river—near the towns of Glendive and Sidney—those communities are very dependent on this industry. As we become familiar with three of the most important economic activities in the Yellowstone River Valley, we will frame our sustainability questions as follows: (a) Are current agricultural practices sustainable? (b) Are current tourism practices sustainable? and (c) Are current oil and gas practices sustainable? Importantly, we might also begin to ask: Can we sustain all three industries into the future?

In Chapter 3, we will examine two elements of environmental sustainability in the Yellowstone River Valley. Each of these concerns brings into focus issues regarding the long-term sustainability of our current environmental practices. To begin, we will examine the situation of the Pallid Sturgeon. This prehistoric fish species is heading toward extinction, but efforts are underway to improve its numbers. Second, we will examine the decline of the cottonwood forests by considering evidence that might make us rethink how we manage flooding in our river bottoms. As we become familiar with these two environmental concerns in the Yellowstone River Valley, we will frame our sustainability questions as follows: (a) Will our current practices allow for the long-term sustainability of the Pallid Sturgeon? and (b) Will our current practices allow for the long-term sustainability of the cottonwood forests? Importantly, we will also ask: What practices need immediate adjustments to sustain these elements of the river valley ecosystem?

Chapter 4 examines elements of social sustainability in the Yellowstone River Valley. We will begin by defining a few important terms, including equality, equity, and environmental justice. From that foundation we will examine scenarios involving public rights and access to public resources. Next, we will examine some mishaps in the oil and gas industry and begin to think about our understandings of fairness in these circumstances. Finally, we will briefly consider the relationships between social sustainability and social stability. As questions of social well-being emerge through these examples, we will begin to see how social sustainability is directly tied to economic and environmental sustainability in the Yellowstone River Valley.

Chapter 5 is designed to illustrate sustainability's complexities. It begins with the topic of water rights and notes that issues arise because many aspects of contemporary water laws, written to suit societal needs of 1872, remain essentially unchanged in principle and execution in contemporary times. It is in this context that we examine the rights of American Indians. Then, we will examine the riparian areas, channel migration processes, and floodplains of the Yellowstone River. We will give attention to the services drawn from healthy riparian areas and to the practices that threaten their health. We note that riparian areas are not fully understood and that they are seldom valued for the full array of benefits they provide humans. Yet, healthy riparian areas are key to the long-term sustainability of the valley. Chapter 5 also highlights the notion of resilience—the ability of environmental and human communities, including businesses, to adapt to stress and change. Readers are encouraged to engage in thoughtful conversations about the complexities associated with trying to improve sustainability and resilience in the valley. We ask: (a) Will current practices concerning water rights allow for sustainability in the Yellowstone River Valley? and (b) Will current practices allow for the long-term health of its riparian areas?

Finally, Chapter 6 shows how detailed attention to sustainability has become a science—sustainability science. In sustainability science, researchers seek to understand complex systems with the intention of intervening to move them toward sustainability. We discuss the central role of communities in sustainability science and how communities of scientists and residents can use resilience to design actions to pursue sustainability.

Inputs From Yellowstone River Valley Residents

In 2006, 2012, and 2018, the authors led investigations into the cultural contours of local interests regarding river issues. They designed an interview protocol that focused on individuals' knowledge of social, ecological, and physical (fluvial) dynamics based on their experiences with the river. They recruited residents throughout the Yellowstone River Valley and interviewed a total of 453 people. During these interviews, residents were encouraged to explain, in their own words, their concerns and hopes for the Yellowstone River and its resources. Known as the Yellowstone River Cultural Inventory (YRCI), detailed summary reports of those confidential interviews are available to the public at the Yellowstone River Clearinghouse. Several scholarly reports were published that include analyses of residents' concerns about ruptured pipelines (Emerson, Hall, and Gilbertz 2021), the strengths drawn from agricultural identities in conservation efforts (Horton et al. 2017), how social power and influence factor into defining ecological goals (Hall et al. 2015), how cultural context affects policy development (Hall et al. 2012), the role of local wisdoms in on-site resource management (Gilbertz et al. 2011), and how local leaders balance managing the interests of the public and individuals concerning this shared environmental resource (Horton et al. 2019).

In 2013 and 2014, the authors were also involved in the design and execution of the Yellowstone Basin water planning efforts led by the Montana Department of Natural Resources and Conservation (DNRC). The water planning efforts involved working directly with the Yellowstone Basin Council to collect and analyze public comments from over 130 valley residents concerning their priorities around water availability, drought readiness, water rights, and state and federal oversight. The team recorded over 100 hours of the council's deliberations. The council's product, the basin plan, is available to the public (Yellowstone River Basin 2014).

In addition, several analytical articles were published examining the basin planning activities, including works addressing the mechanisms for successful stakeholder engagement (Hall et al. 2021), the degree to which scientific and technical data informed decision making (Gilbertz et al. 2019), the role of prior appropriations doctrine as an aid and a hinderance to deliberations

(Anderson et al. 2018), the policy implications of organizing public inputs at local verses basinwide scales (Ward et al. 2017), the strategic implications of introducing "shared giving" as a forward-looking planning option (Anderson et al. 2016), and the value of gathering qualitative research data during public participation events and deliberations (Hall et al. 2016).

Finally, in 2015 and 2016, confidential interviews were conducted in eastern Montana with more than 30 residents for the purpose of understanding the impacts of oil and gas development on local communities. While those interviews have not been summarized as public reports, they have served as the basis for an analysis of local risk perceptions (McEvoy et al. 2017) and for an examination of eastern Montana as an unlikely example of planetary urbanization (Gilbertz, Anderson, and Adkins 2021).

From the tens of thousands of comments gathered over the last 15 years, some confidential and some public in nature, we have selected a few quotes for each chapter that illustrate how comments from residents of the valley expose concerns related to fundamental sustainability issues. Their comments are presented to maintain confidentiality for all, with indications of where in the valley the person resided, the year the comment was made, and the residents' primary stakeholder affiliation.

Often, residents' comments only imply sensitivities to sustainability concerns, but at times the connections are remarkable. Thus, we end Chapter 1 and launch our exploration of sustainability's central question with this quote from a farmer who was asked to describe his long-term goals:

> I have a certain amount of estate that I can hand to my kids. But just think about it, two or three generations beyond, no one's going to scarcely remember me. But, if they can go down to the river and stand on that bank, and I did something positive that helped set the stage to keep that river intact, what a legacy. That's how we have got to view it. That way, or it will go away … [if] people just keep gnawing at the fringes and the edges of it … I mean the river is such a grand place. Yeah, we haven't reached that danger point. I hope that we can somehow do all the right things, so that in four or five or ten generations they're still going to call it the Crown-Jewel-River of the country. Wouldn't that be something? (Farmer near Miles City 2006)

Discussion Questions

1. In what ways have local and regional industries already changed their practices to improve the long-term profitability and economic well-being of our communities?
2. In what ways have advocacy groups influenced society to adopt practices that will improve the environmental sustainability of our communities?
3. In what ways have public calls for action moved society to adopt practices that will improve social sustainability of communities?
4. How do comments made by the farmer near Miles City illustrate sensitivity to sustainability's central question?

Easy Access Resources

Interactive Map Yellowstone River Cumulative Effects Analysis and the Yellowstone River: http://montana.maps.arcgis.com/apps/webappviewer/index.html?id=3fc5b219f4494ebab2477e93a5bbecca

Montana Maps: www.google.com/search?rlz=1C1GCEU_enUS821US827&tbm=isch&sa=1&ei=nSvfXIinNemA0wLLtLu4Bg&q=montanan+maps&oq=montana+maps&gs_l=img.3...7470996.7474389..7474597...0.0..0.90.838.13......2....1..gws-wiz-img.....0..35i39j0i67j0j0i10j0i5i10i30j0i24j0i10i24.G4sMtDlRPb8

Population Statistics, United States: https://suburbanstats.org/

Three Pillars of Corporate Sustainability, explained by Andrew Beattie: https://www.investopedia.com/articles/investing/100515/three-pillars-corporate-sustainability.asp

USGS Publications Warehouse: https://pubs.er.usgs.gov/

Watershed Maps: www.google.com/search?rlz=1C1GCEU_enUS821US827&q=Yellowstone+River+Watershed+map+USGS&tbm=isch&source=univ&sa=X&ved=2ahUKEwi7gYyO4aPiAhXI3J4KHVl5D5MQ7Al6BAgJEBE&biw=1600&bih=1057

Yellowstone River Data Clearinghouse: http://geoinfo.msl.mt.gov/data/yellowstone_river/about

CHAPTER 2

Economic Well-Being in the Yellowstone River Valley

Introduction

We operate in a capitalistic society; thus, the economic well-being of the Yellowstone River Valley is defined by the long-term profitability of existing and future industries, services, and other income-generating activities. In general, people do not engage in economic activities that are not profitable because they cannot afford to do so. Put simply by Beattie (2019), "To be sustainable, a business must be profitable" (3).

Over the past 20 years, concerted efforts have gone toward incorporating sustainability goals into business strategies (Dyllick and Hockerts 2002), especially in the context of international supply chains (Mani and Delgado 2019). While it is not surprising to find businesses and industries that are now moving their practices toward better environmental and social sustainability, it is still true that an engaged sustainability business agenda is difficult to maintain (Dyllick and Muff 2016), and profitability remains the key corporate concern (Svensson and Wagner 2015). However, research shows that complex sustainability initiatives are more likely to be successful when employed as a component of a formal business model (Schaltegger, Hansen, and Lüdeke-Freund 2015). Today, it is argued that business sustainability is most successful when managers and engineers collaborate, both within single businesses and as industrywide agendas (Machado and Davim 2020).

In the Yellowstone River Valley, there are many elements that define the local industries and economies. We focus on elements related to a few key resources (Knox and Marston 2016): cultivable lands, water, energy reserves, and "experience" possibilities (sites and activities that generate memorable events). These four resources are key within the local economies, and all four are easily recognized as being dependent on the Yellowstone River—irrigation, drilling processes, hydraulic fracturing, hunting, fishing, birding, and boating are all activities associated with river resources.

In this chapter, we will first examine agricultural industries, which have been important to the valley for over 100 years. In fact, in 1905, the Huntley Project just east of Billings was authorized by the Department of the Interior. Designed to irrigate over 27,000 acres of land, it was one of the first major federal irrigation projects in the American West (Dick 1996). Today, hundreds of thousands of acres are under cultivation in the Yellowstone River Valley, and the productivity of these lands is dependent on resources such as the soils and the water pulled from the Yellowstone River. These agricultural lands would not be nearly as productive without the water coming from the Yellowstone River, and no examination of the economies of the valley could ignore agricultural practices (Figure 2.1).

Figure 2.1 Harvest time in the valley

Tourism is a second important economy in the state and the valley (Grau 2018). While the river corridor offers many recreational activities for individuals living in the valley, an abundance of people come to the valley from outside Montana, and even from outside the United States, to enjoy recreational experiences, such as fishing, floating, bird watching, bird hunting, and photography. Park County, one of the gateways to YNP, is perhaps the most dependent on tourism. The towns of Livingston and Gardiner are heavily trafficked in the summer by out-of-state visitors who come for the beauty and uniqueness of YNP. Visitors are also drawn to Paradise Valley, which runs from Livingston to Gardiner, and they infuse the area with money every summer. They even support drift-boat builders who charge tens of thousands of dollars for their custom-designed products (Figure 2.2).

Figure 2.2 Drift boat builder's shop

The third area of economic activity in the valley we will examine is oil and gas development in eastern Montana (Figure 2.3). This extractive industry is responsible for producing and transporting oil and gas resources from one of the largest energy reserves in North America, the Bakken oil field. This industry has historically, albeit periodically, played an important role in eastern Montana (Hennip 1973). While oil and gas development creates boom-and-bust cycles for these communities, there is little doubt this industry is an important part of the economy of eastern Montana.

Figure 2.3 Cricket pump in Eastern Montana

Of course, there are other economic activities in the Yellowstone River Valley. However, agriculture, tourism, and the oil and gas industry are three of the most important ones. As we move through this material, keep in mind the key question of economic sustainability: Can we meet our current economic needs without compromising the ability of future generations to meet their economic needs?

Long-Term Profitability of Agricultural Activities

The valley has historically been dependent on numerous agricultural and related industries. Hay, wheat, corn, sorghum, sugar beets, and numerous pulse crops, such as lentils and peas, are grown in the valley. There are no major dams on the Yellowstone River, but there are numerous diversion facilities that allow water to pool and then to be drawn into irrigation canals. Throughout the valley, the river is considered essential to the agricultural community (Gilbertz, Horton, and Hall 2006). The productivity of hundreds of thousands of acres is enhanced by water from the Yellowstone River, and it allows for the long-term profitability of the farms and ranches of the valley. As explained by a family matriarch living near the confluence with the Missouri River, the Yellowstone River is essential and beloved:

> It's a beautiful place to live. We thoroughly enjoy the river, and we talk about it all the time [because] it's really our lifeblood. We have to have that river to irrigate. And, it's our recreation, and we just love the river so much. (Farmer near Fairview 2018)

Over 100 miles away, a different farmer said:

> It's my lifeblood ... We would be devastated without the Yellowstone River, and we would fight to the death to keep it. It's important. Gotta have it ... Farming is a business. It's an enterprise, it has to be profitable. That Yellowstone makes me profitable because it guarantees me a crop. If I will do the things that I need to do—plant, fertilize, build my soils, treat this ground right—it will treat us very good in the process. And it has. (Farmer near Terry 2018)

In the lower river valley, near Glendive and Sidney, the farms are especially productive, and the landscape is dominated by cultivated fields. In fact, farm earnings in this area are estimated as 9 to 14 percent of local earnings in these counties (U.S. Army Corps of Engineers and Yellowstone River Conservation District Council 2015, 1363). However, these figures represent only a portion of the total economic input of agriculture to the local communities. These numbers do not account for the earnings of implement dealers, fuel providers, or suppliers selling agricultural products, such as fertilizers and pesticides. Thus, even though the data indicate that governmental and mining activities add more to the local economies than do agricultural earnings (Serbina and Donovan 2015), because of the dominance of agricultural activities on the local landscape, it is not inaccurate for locals to view themselves as living in farming communities. To this point, locals refer to the Lower Yellowstone Project as proof of the importance of agricultural activities.

Known as Intake, the impressive Lower Yellowstone Project is an irrigation facility, established in 1909. It is located a few miles northeast of Glendive (Reach D8), and it provides irrigation water to over 58,000 acres of farmland (U.S. Bureau of Reclamation n.d.a). At Intake, the river is mostly in one large channel, with one notable sandbar and one side-channel to the south. The irrigation infrastructure includes flow-diversion mechanisms that keep the river in one channel. The irrigation canal runs north, away from the river. As do most such systems in the valley, this irrigation system depends on gravity and the carefully designed slopes of the canals, fields, ditches, and drains for dispersal of the water. To get water onto a field, farmers open floodgates, and water from a canal or a ditch flows across their fields. Later, farmers close the floodgates, and a few days after that, they will open the floodgates again.

As a result of irrigation, a tremendous amount of water flows across the landscape annually from May until September. Images of the valley (Reaches D11 and D12) illustrate that within a few miles downriver of Intake, the amount of irrigated farmland begins to expand across the landscape, mostly to the west of the river. Further downriver (Reaches D14, D15, and D16), we find even greater swaths of cultivated land. In these images, the latest generation of pivot sprinkler systems also become apparent on the landscape as circles or half-circles of green. Pivot systems are much more efficient than flood irrigation practices in terms of water use. Some farmers are switching to these systems because they can calibrate water use to only apply enough water to maintain healthy plants. The water savings are often used to expand the total acreage under cultivation, which in turn should enhance profitability. Yet, as explained by an irrigation equipment supplier, the expansion represents a potential threat:

> I don't think we've seen a conflict yet as far as the use of the water, but you will down the road. We're seeing more and more irrigation systems put in every year. It used to be flood irrigation, where they flood mainly the valleys, but now they've gone to a sprinkler irrigation system, so now they're irrigating the hills several hundred feet above the river. (Pump and dredge supplier in Glendive 2006)

The expanding irrigation activities in this area are noticeable on the landscape near Glendive and Sidney. By comparison, upriver in Prairie County, there is little irrigation infrastructure, and the landscape is quite dry (Reach C1). In this area, many families are primarily engaged in ranching operations, using thousands of acres as grazing pastures (Figure 2.4). Unlike in the eastern United States, where grazing capacity is measured in terms of cows per acre, in the arid Yellowstone River Valley, grazing capacity is measured in terms of acres per cow.

Figure 2.4 Dryland ranching near Columbus, MT

Notably, flood irrigation is still the dominant practice, and it has some important benefits. Much of the water that is diverted from the river for flood irrigation is not used by the plants, and the unused water is not wholly lost. Rather, it soaks into the soil and recharges shallow aquifers. These aquifers store water, and they feed water back toward the river through subsurface gravels. These shallow aquifers also serve many of the homes in the valley (Gilbertz, Hall, and Ward 2013). Thus, sprinkler systems are not without controversy. They are efficient irrigation systems, but if too many of the farmers stop flood irrigation as their primary practice, the water wells in the valley will go dry. Then, water supplies for livestock and for human consumption may also decline.

It is obvious that irrigated lands are much more productive than lands that are not irrigated. Local producers are dependent on the river water for both their yearly and long-term profitability. Unfortunately, and perhaps alarmingly, it is known that the water supply is already overallocated, meaning that if every water-right holder on the Yellowstone River exercises their full measure of water rights, there will not be enough water to satisfy all of the legitimate users (Yellowstone River Basin 2014). Current practices have not led to dire outcomes, but many people worry that running out of water is "just around the corner," especially if drought conditions are intense or protracted. How the overallocation can happen without running out of water is a function of many users not yet taking their full allocations, a circumstance of "paper rights" verses "use rights" (Anderson et al. 2016).

It is also important to note that nearly every farmer in the region uses chemical fertilizers and pesticides to increase crop yields. Because the investments in terms of monetary costs and effort have been proven to increase profitability, the use of fertilizers and pesticides has increased substantially over the years. An industry watchdog reports that in 1960, nitrogen application averaged 17 pounds per acre, per year. This use peaked in 2007 at a rate of over 82 pounds per acre, per year (Gro Intelligence 2018). Because these applications are expensive, it is fair to assume that most farmers are careful in how they use such chemicals:

> I don't want to hurt anything. For one, it costs me money to waste fertilizer and pesticide ... We put just enough on to grow the crop we want, and that's it. And not only that, on sugar beets if you put too much on, you'll get no sugar content. So, you don't over-put it on. You put just the right amount. You want it to grow good until August, and then you want it to peter out. (Farmer near Sidney 2018)

Not only do farmers not want to use more than they need (Figure 2.5), some of these same farmers express concerns about the impacts of the chemicals:

> That's another thing that's gone, the bees ... You know, they're out in the daytime, and guys spray, and then that kills them immediately. This [neighbor] has these bees, and when we spray, we always let him know. And he says, 'Well, you can spray in the morning until about 10. So, we always get up right before about five [to spray with that] big old sprayer... That's what I attribute it [the lack of bees] to. (Farmer between Hysham and Forsyth 2018)

Later, another farmer said, "I'm worried about the bees. I decided to try to something. So, I ordered $5,000 worth of wildflower seeds. If people knew I did that, they would think I was crazy." (Farmer Telling Secrets 2018)

Figure 2.5 Irrigated farmland

The farmers are also aware that many of the applied chemicals are washed away by rains and successive irrigation and that the chemicals can enter the river, directly or indirectly as nonpoint source pollution. In general, it is assumed that water pollution in eastern Montana follows the national trends. Namely, the leading sources of pollutants to the streams and rivers of the United States come from agricultural activities (U.S. Environmental Protection Agency n.d.a). The Environmental Protection Agency (EPA) explicitly lists agricultural activities as a key source of groundwater contamination (U.S. Environmental Protection Agency n.d.b), and runoff from treated fields is known to contaminate many of our rivers and streams (U.S. Environmental Protection Agency 2019). In some regions of the United States, other industries would be likely sources of contamination. However, nationwide, the lack of safe drinking water is, in great measure, a result of upriver agricultural practices.

Water quality is managed through the Clean Water Act. Among other things, the Clean Water Act deals with nonpoint source pollution. Efforts to address pollution are implemented in accordance with the federally mandated Total Maximum Daily Load (TMDL) Program. In the Yellowstone River Valley, the TMDL process has been triggered by nitrate levels associated with nonpoint source pollution, assumed to come from nearby agricultural fields. Water quality tests indicate that seven sections of the river and its tributaries violate federal standards (Montana Department of Environmental Quality 2020). As a means of reducing the costs associated with fertilizers, and (perhaps) to avoid water contamination, new techniques for rotating crops have been adopted by some farmers. This means the farmers alternate types of plantings, and thereby they use the natural resources of different plants, like nitrogen-fixers (e.g., legumes), to replenish certain nutrients to the soils. These rotations are helping reduce the use of fertilizers, but they have a limited capacity in terms of amending overworked soils, especially when farmers are increasingly including second plantings in each growing season. Nearly every farmer in eastern Montana depends on irrigation, fertilizers, and pesticides to boost their yields and to generate long-term profitability for their individual farm operation. Keeping the nutrients and chemicals where they are needed is in the best interest of everyone who depends on the river.

Long-Term Profitability of Tourism

Fishing, boating, camping, and hunting along the river have long been favorite recreational activities of the people of the valley and of visitors. The 60 miles between Livingston and the Roosevelt Arch at Gardiner is a favored route to YNP. From 1882 until 1959, the Northern Pacific Railroad ran passenger links into the park, with the Livingston terminal having a monopoly on such travels for several decades. The historic Italianate style of the Livingston Depot, designed by the architects of New York's Grand Central Station, welcomed train passengers with open arms (Livingston Depot Foundation n.d.). Today, it is restored to its grand beauty and is used as a special events venue, but for nearly 80 years it served as the beginning point for thousands of visitors' adventures to YNP. They came from all over the United States and the world (Museum of the Yellowstone n.d.). Then, and today, the route from Livingston to YNP proceeds through the area known as Paradise Valley.

With mountain ranges on each side of the valley, and the Yellowstone River bisecting the terrain, there is every reason to call it Paradise (Figure 2.6). Indeed, Paradise Valley is spectacular in every season, and even though passenger rail service to YNP is no longer available, Paradise Valley's sweeping views of cottonwood forests, grazing cattle, and river crossings between the snow-capped Absaroka and Gallatin mountain ranges remains a popular passage. Adding to its appeal, the Boulder River and other sites near Livingston were used in 1991 for filming the movie *A River Runs Through It*. As one local explained, "Ever since that movie, we're on the map. People from all over the world come here to fish" (Owner of Fly-Fishing Shop in Livingston 2006).

Figure 2.6 Paradise Valley in October

As an important corridor for people to enter and exit YNP, Paradise Valley has become dependent on tourism dollars, and the valley is especially busy with recreational activities during the summer months. As explained in an analysis of traffic in the valley, the number of vehicles on Highway 89 doubles in July as compared with January (Peccia 2013). In 2019, Montana's Park County was home to approximately 16,600 residents, half of whom resided in the town of Livingston (U.S. Census Bureau 2019a). Of special interest in Park County's economy, is the number of jobs attributed to nonresident travel. In Park County, in 2014, nonresident spending generated $124.1 million in direct economic activity and another $45.8 million in indirect activity. The top four expenditures by nonresident visitors were fuel, restaurants and bars, lodging, and outfitters and guides (Sage 2016). One can calculate that nonresident spending supported well over 2,000 jobs, either directly or indirectly, and that well over 20 percent of the Park County workforce is earning income based on nonresident travel.

It is possible to visit this area in the fall when one seems to have the valley to oneself; however, innumerable rafts, canoes, and drift boats line the river in an almost bumper-to-bumper fashion during the summer season. In addition to kids on innertubes, high-dollar tourists arrive for dream vacations. These are people who can afford to fly into the area on private jets, who are able to spend $5,000 per day having a local fishing guide teach them how to catch trout, and who might order a $20,000 custom drift boat for their next visit (Gilbertz, Emerson, and Hall 2020). On a hot summer day, there is seemingly no limit to the number of boats or people on the river. One young fishing guide, who had been in the business for five years, noted the increasing summer recreational pressures:

> Just in my short guiding career, there is definitely more people on the river. And I don't know really why that is … Probably one out of the ten boats I see in the summer is a fishing guide. Most of them are just splash and giggle people, as we call them—rafts and party barges. (Young Fishing Guide in Livingston 2018)

In the summer, a visit to Paradise Valley is a highly socialized encounter, especially because even though the number of visitors increases each year, there are only a few designated facilities for launching watercraft. A veteran guide explained the increasing traffic this way:

> I don't want to work on weekends, but I've gone up there to do caretaking chores. And if you look upstream from the Mill Creek Bridge, you can see twenty-five floating things up there, and twenty-five floating things down there … Stand-up paddleboards, and kayaks, and rubber duckies, and … the thing I'm seeing now is

> the really giant raft with the big sun-awning over the top … And there's six or eight people in the raft … You look around, and you realize the overall pressure. The fish do react when twenty boats run over their heads in a day, and in some of those stretches, it's just getting to be pretty crazy. I was shocked. I took a client up to Carbella [boat launch] last week … It's already the first week of October, and it was actually not a terribly great day—kind of cold and windy. And I thought there … won't be any recreational floaters up here … [I thought] there might be another guide or two. And while I was rigging my boat, probably six guide boats came in … And then, late in the afternoon when I thought nobody would be putting in, I saw three or four more boats come past us. (Veteran Fishing Guide in Livingston 2018)

The public boat launches are busier and busier, in part because, unless one has the express permission from the landowner, it is not legal to cross private property to gain access to the river. With the river in sight from nearly every vantage throughout Paradise Valley, and with hundreds of thousands of visitors to the area each year, trespass issues involving visitors attempting to access the river across private lands are regularly reported in the local news (Cramer 2020). One result of the access issue is that many of the full-time residents of Paradise Valley are engaged in hybrid operations, whereby they subsidize their agricultural incomes with enterprises that capture tourist dollars. For instance, several ranches with properties on the banks of the Yellowstone River provide fee-based access to the river, and in some families, the younger adults provide fishing guide services that more than double the family income when compared with the income generated by agricultural activities.

For the most part, the towns and settlements of Paradise Valley depend on the summer season to provide enough income to survive the winters, and local sensitivities to this economy manifest as ambivalence. On one hand, summer tourism provides immediate and long-term profitability, even for businesses such as the local bookstores, which tend to cater to readers looking for novels set in Montana. On the other hand, tourists are not always respectful of local customs, nor are they knowledgeable of Montana laws. Locals look forward to, and dread, the summer season.

In the summer of 2016, the Montana Department of Fish, Wildlife, and Parks temporarily closed recreational access to the Yellowstone River in Paradise Valley, and many people in the county were affected financially (Montana Fish, Wildlife and Parks 2016b). Fishing guides, boat rental shops, restaurants, and hotels saw their summer revenues drop. The closing was in response to a sudden fish kill that resulted in hundreds of dead fish washing onto the banks of the Yellowstone River. Laboratory tests confirmed that there was an outbreak of proliferative kidney disease (PKD). It was theorized that because fish are particularly vulnerable to PKD when they are stressed, the river itself had contributed to the outbreak. There had been much less rain than normal in the summer of 2016, and greater-than-usual amounts of irrigation water had been drawn off the river. The drop in water level led to record-breaking low flows, and, as a result, water temperatures rose and stressed the fish. It is widely held that in their weakened condition, the fish were more susceptible to PKD than during typical summers. The parasite associated with PKD is always present in the river, so not everyone agreed with the theory that flows, temperatures, and irrigation led to the PDK outbreak. But regardless of the cause, the outcome was that the recreational economy was forced to suspend activities. Some members of the community voiced concerns that climate change was now affecting Paradise Valley and that business as usual was at risk. The veteran guide offered this comment:

> Everybody seems to be asking, as guides and outfitters, do we do our jobs the same as we did ten years ago, or twenty years ago? And the answer is, definitely no … Our industry has really had to change in some fairly dramatic ways … I certainly read enough to recognize the signs of climate change, but I thought that's in the future … People who have grandkids, their grandkids are sure going to have to deal with that issue. And I guess I've been somewhat shocked to realize that a decade later we are dealing with it pretty much on a day-to-day basis … I used to [take] lots and lots of phone calls from people saying, "When should I come to Montana?" The answer I gave them in 1995 is not the answer I would give them now. (Veteran Fishing Guide in Livingston 2018)

The economic impacts of the 2016 closure on Paradise Valley communities illustrated the importance of recreational opportunities for the local economy, and fishing guides were affected directly. Many of the local fishing guides accepted the closure as necessary to their long-term profitability (Chaney 2016); however, it was an immediate hardship and potentially a long-term profitability risk. The fishing guides began to wonder: What if drought conditions are worse next season? If we have another dry year, will there be another fish kill and another suspension of recreational activities? And how many guides can survive if fish kills become a common summer occurrence? The closure also revealed the vulnerability of communities throughout the greater Yellowstone River Valley who also depend on tourism and outdoor recreation for their economic sustainability.

Those who earn their living as guides and outfitters also wonder how the overall popularity of the river might change their industry. It might be possible to add boat launch facilities to accommodate the ever-increasing numbers of visitors, but what would the consequences of having even more people on the river be? Recreational managers have begun considering ways to control recreational access to the river in Paradise Valley (French 2020), and outfitters are wondering how that will affect their profits. They have seen the financial impacts of controlled access on the people who make their living by bringing tourists out into nature.

An example that illustrates the financial impacts of limiting access to a popular recreational location is that of the Smith River of Montana. The Smith River is a 59-mile river that flows north through central-western Montana, draining water from the Big Belt and Little Belt Mountains to the upper Missouri River. As the popularity of this river grew, the crowds prevented the peaceful enjoyment of nature and most users agreed that the quality of the recreational experience was greatly diminished. In 1989, the Smith River Management Act was enacted, and the state now defines how many people have access to the river each year. The state also limits use to only rafts, canoes, kayaks, and drift boats. The state employs a lottery system for dispensing access permits. The permits are relatively inexpensive, but the chances of drawing a permit are less and less each year. With 10,866 applications, "the Smith River experienced record-setting interest and visitation again in 2020" (Kluz 2021, 2). Trout

Unlimited, a nonprofit conservation organization, reported that "the odds percentage of getting a permit in the lottery during the high-use season is now in the single digits" (Montana Trout Unlimited 2021). They also noted that outfitters, who previously paid no fees, now "pay $200/trip."

If, as is the case in the Smith River, access in Paradise Valley becomes more expensive and permits are not announced until mid-February, outfitters and guides will need to adjust how they conduct business. They might not be able to accommodate loyal customers by booking their next trip a year in advance. They may also begin to face opposition in terms of use rights if the public feels they get more than their share (Danylchuk, Tiedemann, and Cooke 2017). From within, many of the local guides and outfitters are examining their practices and attempting to maintain the highest degree of recreational ethics, for both personal and business reasons:

> As a guide, my level of river etiquette is maybe on a little bit higher level, I would like to think. And, this is speaking for all guides, I would hope. You know, I really try to give people their space. If you see a guy who doesn't have guide stickers, just let him fish. Don't try to cut him off. He's not doing it every day. You don't want to get a bad rep—especially me, being a young guide. And I work for other people, I don't want to tarnish their name … And, I grew up here. I've family that's been here for 100 years. So, you know, I care about protecting, keeping my office clean. There was one instance this summer, I was guiding, there were four or five of us guides, and we all had clients. It was a big corporate group … We pull over for lunch, and one of the fishermen in my buddy's boat took a beer bottle and threw it over his shoulder onto the beach. And luckily it was a sandy beach, so it didn't break. And the guides all just kind of looked at each other. Then my buddy Jeremy was like, "I'll go get that." And he set the bottle in his cooler. And, another one of my friends that was guiding said, "Hey, bud, how would you like it if someone came and threw a beer bottle in your office?" You know, so we try to keep it clean, because we're trying to impress people with the area, so they come back. (Young Fishing Guide in Livingston 2018)

In Paradise Valley, economic and environmental sustainability are inextricably intertwined.

Long-Term Profitability of Oil and Gas Development

While it may seem odd to consider nonrenewable resources in a sustainability discussion, considering the not-yet-curbed consumptive habits of the country, this third sector of the economy of the Yellowstone River Valley, oil and gas development, remains important to the valley. As we did when considering agriculture, here we focus on the areas near the lower reaches of the river where, in the 1950s, the first oil wells in Montana were drilled. At that time, oil and gas were mostly being pulled from the Dakota formation, a geologic stratum rich with petroleum reserves (Hennip 1973). The most recent oil and gas boom in Montana involves the Bakken geological formation (Figure 2.7). While much of the Bakken field is located under western North Dakota, it also lies under northeastern Montana (U.S. Geological Survey 2013). The Bakken field is important to the entire United States because its total petroleum reserve is estimated to be one of the largest in the country. Some estimate this reserve as potentially sufficient to provide the United States with three years of energy independence—making the Bakken an extremely important petroleum reserve (DiLallo 2018).

The entire reserve is not recoverable (U.S. Geological Survey n.d.a). The Bakken field is approximately one mile underground and is made of tightly compressed shales. Current technologies cannot extract all the oil and gas held in the Bakken shales. In 2013, the United States Geological Survey (USGS) estimated that of hundreds of billions of barrels in the field, only a fraction, 7.4 billion barrels, were recoverable (U.S. Geological Survey 2013). However, by 2018, Continental Resources, the largest oil and gas producer in the Bakken, estimated that 30 to 40 billion barrels were recoverable (Scheid 2018). The new estimate is based on successful uses of hydraulic fracturing and horizontal drilling as recovery processes.

Anecdotal evidence of the anticipated long-term profitability of developing the Bakken field is found in the number of companies operating in the area. Nearly 40 companies were recently listed as active developers (Bakken Shale n.d.). Five producers dominate production: Continental

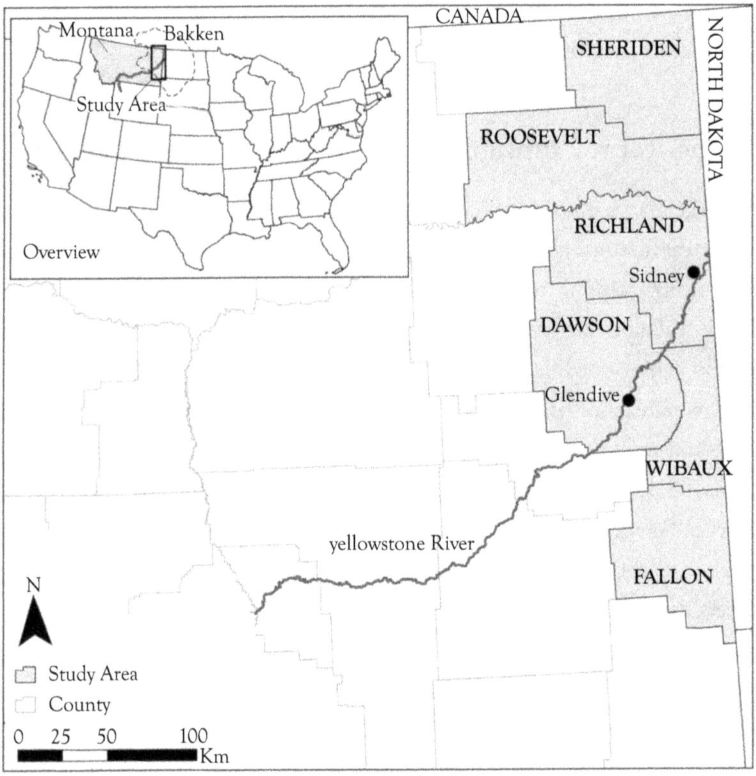

Figure 2.7 Map of Montana with Bakken counties (shaded)

Source: Gilbertz, Anderson, and Adkins 2020

Resources, EOG Resources, ExxonMobil, Hess, and Whiting Petroleum. These five producers operate internationally, and together they control nearly three million acres of leased minerals in the Bakken field (DiLallo 2016). They operate in Montana when oil and gas markets make production in the Bakken profitable, and they pause operations when the markets slow.

Over the years, the counties in eastern Montana periodically experienced "booms" in oil and gas development. These booms were followed, each time, by a "bust" economy. Some locals are rather casual in how they describe the economic ups and downs caused by oil and gas development: "Agriculture is our stabilizing industry. And where you have the oil influence, and well developments, that comes and goes on a cycle of ten years.

So, we're on a growth spurt now, again" (Public Works Official in Sidney 2006). Many people in this part of the valley argue that their communities have profited from "good" boom cycles, and they report few concerns regarding the risks associated with oil and gas development (McEvoy et al. 2017). The booms are considered helpful in terms of employment and revenue to local businesses, even though the unevenness of the benefits over the years is also worthy of comment:

> [The oil and gas industry brings us] a lot of jobs. Brings more business to town, and everybody gains—a lot of people gain, grocery stores and hotels. They bring a lot of money into the community … It makes the economy better, pretty much … [But with] this last boom, we pay more for tires. Everything went up. Groceries. Everything went up. Ninety percent of the people actually didn't gain anything, but there are some people that did … Them other booms were small. There's probably very little benefit, actually, when you think about it. The jail costs more, all our goods went up. A few people made money, [and] some local businesses did very well. But overall, it's probably not that great. (Farmer near Glendive 2016)

Some benefits to the economy are measured by the public projects funded by oil and gas tax revenues. In 2018, a Commissioner from Richland County listed examples of new county infrastructure projects that had been paid for using county revenues from oil and gas development:

> The county, to date, has put $45 million into directly affecting the city [of Sidney], and total, through the county, is $66 million. And that's all from oil. And the beautiful thing about this is, there is no property tax that was associated with it. None of this has been paid for by the taxpayer. It's all been paid for by oil severance monies. Every bit of it. That is, in my opinion, pretty good management on our part. We just got done with the senior citizens' center/fire hall … for $2,200,000. They didn't have to pass a bond; they didn't have to raise anybody's property taxes to pay for

> this ... We are not in debt. We paid for this stuff as we went ... We put $1.3 million in ... streets and sidewalk upgrades. We just put a new sewer system in [the town of] Savage, as a matter of fact, for $650,000. All of that is cash money from the oil and gas monies. (Richland County Commissioner in Sidney 2018)

An important issue in the oil and gas industry is the need for water. As was true in the 1950s, oil and gas production requires the use of water to lubricate the drilling process. Today, each well drilled in the Bakken will descend approximately one mile. Then, with horizontal drilling, the boring will likely proceed another mile, or even two additional miles. Drilling muds, which are prepared with local water, are used as lubrication throughout the drilling process. Even more water is required to hydraulically fracture wells, a process that is especially needed in wells with horizontal sections. Highly pressurized "fracking" fluids, which are mostly water, are injected into wells to crack the compressed shale formation and release the oil and gas. The USGS estimates that across the United States, each oil and gas well requires anywhere from 1 to 16 million gallons of water for successful fracturing (U.S. Geological Survey n.d.b). The range is broad because of significant differences in the depth and length of wells across the United States.

To address this need for local water in the drilling process, water depots appeared on the landscape in eastern Montana during the Bakken boom. These depots sold water to the oil and gas producers. Also, some farmers sought to sell water originally designated for irrigation to oil companies in need of water for drilling purposes. In some cases, irrigation water was, perhaps illegally, hauled to drilling rigs. On an outing near the confluence with the Missouri River, a local made an off-hand comment about a passing truck. When asked for an explanation, the local clarified by describing a potentially illegal practice, "He's not supposed to be doing that ... He was filling his water tanks for the rigs right out of the irrigation ditch" (Local Historian in Fairview 2018).

Specific to the Bakken field, an industry report stated that most oil and gas wells in this region use one to five million gallons of water (Energy and Environmental Research Center n.d.), some of which is permanently removed from the system. While the water used for the fracturing process can be recovered, the processes for treating the water to rid it of chemicals and contamination are expensive. Most of the used water for fracking in the Bakken field is permanently disposed of by injecting it into abandoned oil and gas wells. Thus, fracking in the Bakken field is generally a consumptive use of water. The used water, known in the industry as industrial wastewater, is hauled to disposal depots or disposal wells where it is removed from the overall system of available water (Figure 2.8). At the peak of production in 2007, the DNRC issued 868 oil drilling permits, the majority of which were for wells in the Bakken field (Montana Board of Oil and Gas Production 2007). One can calculate that the resulting need for water assuredly exceeded 800 million gallons in that single year.

Figure 2.8 Disposal depot in Bakken region

The town of Sidney, home to fewer than 6,000 people, is nonetheless subject to economic cycles resulting from global industrial forces. Decisions by the Organization of the Petroleum Exporting Countries, which includes Saudi Arabia, Iran, Iraq, and Venezuela, will determine whether oil production in the Bakken booms or busts. Widely known in eastern Montana is this: when the price of oil drops, their communities feel it. Moreover, careful analyses have even shown that, over the long run, these boom-and-bust cycles do not generally benefit the local communities or their economies (Haggerty et al. 2014). Other studies have shown that only a few individuals in the local community are focused on the exploitive aspects of development spurred by transnational corporations and global dynamics (Gilbertz, Anderson, and Adkin 2020). Even so, these things are clear: the boom-and-bust nature of the industry is unlikely to change, and with each drilling boom, demands for water will spike too.

The three economic sectors of the valley examined in this chapter force us to think about how these practices should proceed: Can we maintain the long-term profitability of these sectors without compromising the ability of future generations to meet their economic needs? All three depend on the resources of the river. Can they all proceed without adaptation, or is it more likely that they will be in competition with one another for water resources?

Discussion Questions

Our brief examination of practices in the lower reaches of the Yellowstone River Valley leaves us with several questions to consider regarding the long-term profitability of agriculture:

1. What factors will allow agriculture to remain a sustainable sector of the economies of Prairie, Dawson, and Richland Counties?
2. Are current practices involving water, fertilizers, and pesticides sustainable? If not, what adjustments should we ask the agricultural community to make?
3. Is it reasonable to ask the agricultural community to risk long-term profitability for the benefit of future generations?

Regarding tourism and fishing near Livingston, we might ask:

1. Will closed recreational access, to save the fish, result in lost jobs throughout the county, temporarily—or even permanently?
2. What can the larger valley learn about economic sustainability from the Paradise Valley fish kill of 2016?

Regarding the oil and gas industry, we ask these sustainability questions:

1. Does oil and gas development constitute a sustainable economy?
2. How do the boom-and-bust cycles diminish the local sustainability of this industry?
3. How do technologies affect the sustainability of the industry?
4. What global factors influence the profitability of oil and gas production in eastern Montana?
5. Is this industry's consumptive use of water a serious concern?

Also:

1. How do the comments from locals concerning agriculture, tourism, and oil and gas development illustrate sensitivity to sustainability's central question?

Easy Access Resources

Fertilizer and Pesticide Use in the United States: https://gro-intelligence.com/insights/a-look-at-fertilizer-and-pesticide-use-in-the-us#Fertilizer

Institute for Tourism and Recreation Research at the University of Montana: https://scholarworks.umt.edu/itrr_pubs/

Nonpoint Source Pollution from Agriculture: www.epa.gov/nps/nonpoint-source-agriculture

United States Bureau of Reclamation—Projects and Facilities: www.usbr.gov/projects/

United States Geological Society, Map of Bakken: https://pubs.usgs.gov/fs/2013/3013/fs2013-3013.pdf

Yellowstone River Basin Water Plan, 2014: http://dnrc.mt.gov/divisions/water/management/docs/state-water-plan/yellowstone/river-basin-plan/yellowstone_river_basin_report_final.pdf

Short: The Yellowstone River Fish-Kill, 2016 https://nps.gov/articles/the-yellowstone-river-fish-kill.htm

Yellowstone River Interactive Map http://montana.maps.arcgis.com/apps/webappviewer/index.html?id=3fc5b219f4494ebab2477e93a5bbecca

CHAPTER 3

Environmental Well-Being in the Yellowstone River Valley

Introduction

We turn our attention to a second key concern for sustainability theory and practice: the long-term well-being of the environment. Our case study leads us to examine two environmental concerns in the Yellowstone River Valley. To begin, we will learn about the Pallid Sturgeon—a federally protected, endangered fish species—and we will examine efforts to save this species. Next, we will look at the cottonwood forests of the valley, where, in some areas, it appears that tree reproduction and growth are not occurring as expected. We will learn why these impressive and much-loved trees are potentially threatened. In both examples, it appears that human practices, especially practices of the 20th century, have affected environmental health and well-being.

Long-Term Well-Being of Pallid Sturgeon

In general, and for some time, conservation biologists have worried that we are losing variety among the species of the Earth (Soulé 1985), and the potential loss of a prehistoric fish species is troubling. Yet today, despite surviving many fluctuations in weather, climate, and harvesting pressures over the ages, some of our oldest fish species are in crisis. The Pallid Sturgeon (*Scaphirhynchus albus*) is one such species. It is a rare fish that appears to be mostly unchanged over 78 million years (Jordan 2013). Sometimes referred to as "living dinosaurs," individual Pallid Sturgeon start small (Figure 3.1), but they often grow to six feet in length and well

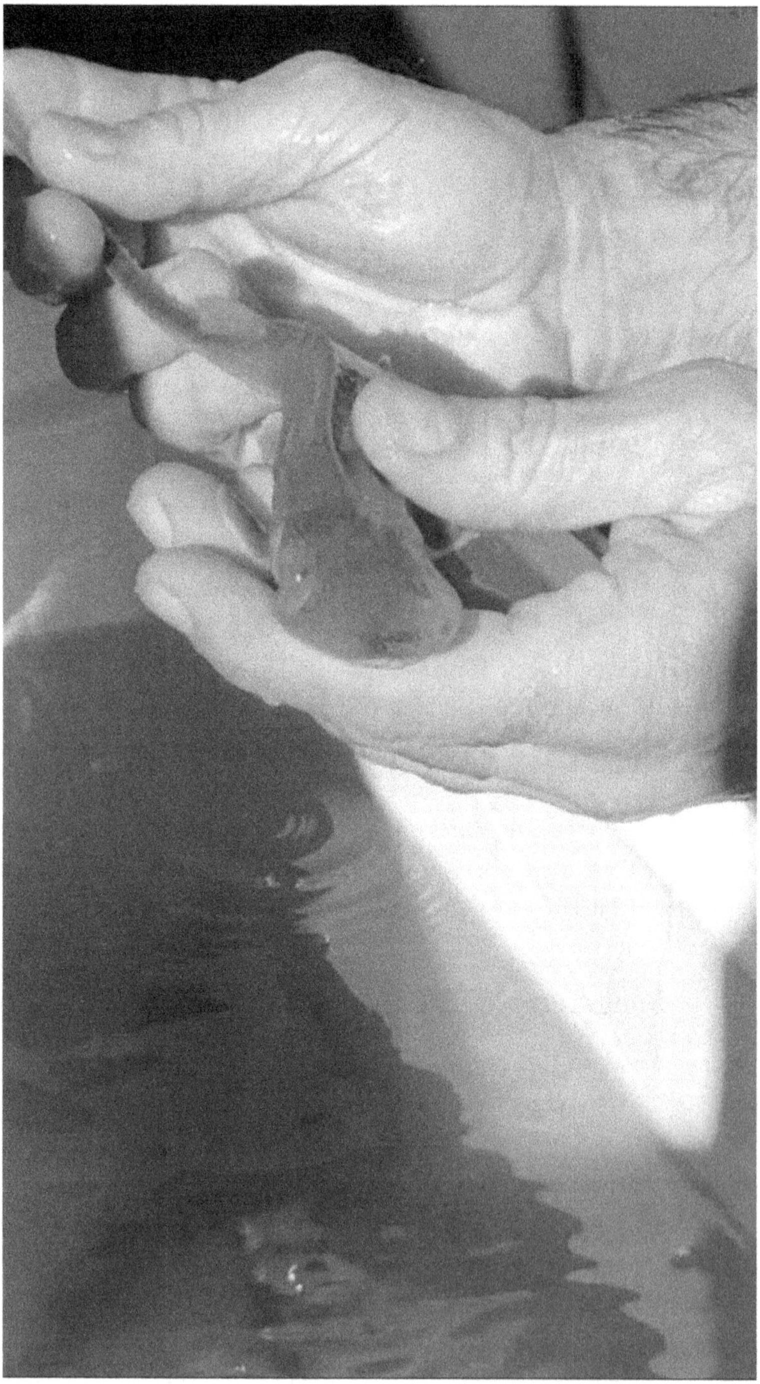

Figure 3.1 Fingerling Pallid Sturgeon at Miles City Hatchery

over 75 pounds, especially those occupying northern habitats, such as near the confluence of the Missouri and Yellowstone Rivers. Even though predatory, they are generally bottom dwellers, moving through the lower murkiness of river waters.

The historical habitat of the Pallid Sturgeon extended from the lower Mississippi River at the Gulf of Mexico into the far reaches of the Upper Missouri (Jordan 2013). Habitat also included the warm-water region of the Yellowstone River, extending from its confluence with the Missouri River in North Dakota to the transition zone (colder waters) near Billings, Montana. In earlier times, Pallid Sturgeon would have also spawned in the Powder and Tongue Rivers (Backes 2020), which are warm-water tributaries that enter the lower Yellowstone River near Terry and at Miles City, respectively (see border of Reaches C21 and D1). In the area of the Yellowstone and Missouri River confluence (Reach D16), these fish do not reach reproductive maturity for over 20 years, and they can live for more than 60 years. The Pallid Sturgeon of the confluence are believed to live, on average, 20 years longer than their cousins in the midwestern and southern states because the winter season in the north is comparatively elongated. It is theorized that the longer periods of cold, and, thus, longer periods of reduced metabolic rates, result in slower development and maturation of the Pallid Sturgeon in Montana (Backes 2020).

Beginning in the 1960s, state and federal biologists noted a sharp decline in the number of Pallid Sturgeon, and in 1990, the species was listed as endangered under the guidelines of the Endangered Species Act (ESA) (Jordan 2013). Federal authorities were required to develop a recovery plan that would account for the primary causes of the population decline and identify specific projects and methods that could reverse the trend. The original recovery plan of 1993 and the revised recovery plan of 2013 identified three factors contributing to the declining populations. Each of these factors resulted from human activities that were begun early in the 20th century without much thought as to how the projects or practices might affect fish species.

The first cause of population decline is attributed to the many reservoirs on the Missouri River system (Jordan 2013). By the 1960s, the Missouri River was essentially held in a series of impoundments, with comparatively little free-flowing river. Moreover, the reservoirs are held in place by dams that forestall fish passage to their historical reaches. Indeed, by 1990, the Missouri River had functioned for more than 30 years as a series of lakes, rather than as a flowing river. Today, with their historical ranges functionally divided, some communities of Pallid Sturgeon have lived in isolation for over 100 years.

Second, efforts to control river channels and to reduce flood potential have led to significant reductions in the number and lengths of side channels (Jordan 2013). Side channels have long been purposefully blocked to avoid flooding on private properties and, often, to claim land that might otherwise be inaccessible to landowners for agricultural or developmental purposes. Even ephemeral channels, those that have water only during the spring, are often blocked. The idea behind blocking side channels is always the same: keep the river contained. The loss of side channels is problematic for the Pallid Sturgeon because the side channels are where spawning occurs and are, therefore, essential for successful reproduction. Also, juveniles need to spend some time in these side channels to build up their strength as swimmers before entering the main channels of larger rivers.

Third, where irrigation water is extracted, fish can be drawn into irrigation canals, a process known as entrainment. Once fish are in the canals, there is virtually no chance of survival (Jordan 2013). Entrainment is an issue for all fish species in the Missouri and Yellowstone Rivers, but when a species is in decline, the entrainments are especially regrettable. Together with the other two human-caused changes, entrainment has negatively affected the habitat range and character, the reproductive success, and the life-expectancies of the Pallid Sturgeon.

In an attempt to stem the precipitous Pallid Sturgeon decline, federal and state agencies began hatching programs. The National Fish Hatchery at Garrison Dam on the Missouri River in North Dakota began collecting wild adult Pallid Sturgeon in 1988. Since then, the hatchery has been breeding adults and raising juveniles (U.S. Fish and Wildlife Service 2020). When released to the wild, the survival rates of these hatchery-raised fish were not particularly good during the early years, but with the introduction of resistance flows in hatchling tanks, the success rates of released juveniles have greatly improved. Another hatchery, the Miles City Fish Hatchery managed by the Montana Department of Fish,

Wildlife and Parks, housed three male Pallid Sturgeon that were each believed to be more than 80 years in age. As denizens of the local domain, these males produced milt (seminal fluid) that was considered especially valuable (Montana Fish, Wildlife and Parks 2016a).

Mike Backes is the senior fish biologist for Pallid Sturgeon recovery in Montana. He lives in the lower valley and has spent more than 30 years studying the Pallid Sturgeon of the area. Recently, he explained that nearly every hatchling from Miles City is electronically tagged and fitted with a transmitter (Backes 2020). This allows biologists to track the released stocks. In fact, some individual Pallid Sturgeons have been monitored for more than 20 years. The biologists even track wild individuals (i.e., those that hatched in the river and not in a hatchery) when they can catch them and fit them with tags and transmitters. In correspondence, Backes explained some of the difficulties in tracking an individual Pallid Sturgeon:

> [This spring] we caught a wild male. He was a priority fish to capture in 2020, [but] catching him was a complete surprise because the transmitter had died and was no longer functioning. We installed a new transmitter and released him. The expected battery life of the new transmitter is eight years. (Michael Backes, e-mail message to Susan Gilbertz, July 06, 2020)

He also mentioned a large female caught by the field team in 2020 (Figure 3.2):

> We sampled an area of the Yellowstone River … to find "Female Code 43." We wanted to determine if she would spawn in 2020. We had intel from other staff that she was in the area. We were lucky enough to find and capture her by using telemetry equipment and a trammel net. She was full of eggs, and she is the largest Pallid Sturgeon I have ever seen. … [Later,] I learned that she actually never spawned and is atretic—reabsorbing the eggs. We have no understanding why she is atretic. This is rarely seen in adult Pallid Sturgeon. (Michael Backes, e-mail message to Susan Gilbertz, July 06, 2020)

Figure 3.2 Tagged Pallid Sturgeon, full of eggs

Photo: Mike Backes

Beyond directing the operation of hatcheries, Pallid Sturgeon recovery plans also identified areas for habitat improvements. The plans noted that, in the northern waters, overall recovery would be enhanced if the Pallid Sturgeon had access to a much greater extent of the warm-water habitats on the Yellowstone River and its warm-water tributaries (Jordan 2013). The recovery plans also called upon river managers to address the fish blockage caused by the irrigation facility at Intake.

You will remember that Intake provides irrigation water to over 58,000 acres of farmland in the lower Yellowstone River Valley (Reach D8). Remember, too, that Intake needs a pool from which it can draw irrigation water. At Intake, a pulley system stretches across the river to deliver rocks across the entire span of the river channel. The rocks, and the wooden "cribs" that they fall into, function as a small dam, a weir. This weir is approximately five feet in height and creates a pool of water on the upriver side of the rocks. Once there is adequate depth in the pool to allow water to flow through the irrigation headgate and into the main irrigation canal, no further rocks are added, and water flows both into the canal and over the rock weir. Each spring, after high waters have torn away at the weir, more rocks are delivered to (again) raise the height of the weir, again to about five feet. Throughout the valley, residents refer to Intake and to similar rock weirs as diversion dams. Intake is the largest diversion dam facility on the Yellowstone River. These weirs do not stop *all* water from flowing downstream, and the Yellowstone River is still known as the longest free-flowing river in the continental United States.

For the Pallid Sturgeon, the rock diversion dam at Intake is generally insurmountable (Jordan 2013). The Pallid Sturgeon, which tend to swim along the bottom of the river, encounter the rock structure and have no instinct for negotiating its height. Thus, even though the river continues to flow, and even though a five-foot rock weir may seem insignificant, it is a blockage for most Pallid Sturgeon. Very few successfully navigate the weir or find their way to the side channel that can afford them access to their historical spawning areas above Intake. Of the few that make it past Intake, even fewer manage to make it to the Powder or Tongue Rivers (Backes 2020).

Local fish biologists play an important role in the Pallid Sturgeon recovery efforts. Not only are their data important to understanding the species but they also show just how rare it is for Pallid Sturgeon to get upriver from Intake. The biologists get excited when they find Pallid Sturgeon upriver from Intake:

> We continue to learn more every year. Two Pallid Sturgeon, a wild male and a juvenile, used the Tongue River this year. They were in the Tongue River for nearly two weeks. This is the first documented use of a Pallid Sturgeon in the Tongue River since an angler caught one in 1950. (Michael Backes, e-mail message to Susan Gilbertz, July 06, 2020)

The biologists are also amazed by certain individuals they have tracked for several years:

> [This spring] a wild female went up the Yellowstone River to within a few miles of … Hathaway. [In the past,] the farthest a female had gone upstream of Intake was the Powder River confluence in 2012. Ironically, it's the same fish. And, she migrated 20 miles up the Powder River in 2014. (Michael Backes, e-mail message to Susan Gilbertz, July 06, 2020)

According to the ESA, once the causes for a population decline are identified, remedies must also be identified and evaluated in terms of costs and potentials for effectiveness. With Intake functioning as a fish blockage, two alternative remedies were given a great deal of attention and consideration. First, a rock ramp was evaluated as a means of helping the Pallid Sturgeon negotiate the height of the rock weir. The idea was to place materials in the river below the weir, creating a gradual incline of small steps to the top of the diversion dam. The Pallid Sturgeon would need pools where they could rest before negotiating each next-higher level, and the overall length of the rock ramp was estimated at over a half mile (Jordon 2013). Second, an enhanced bypass channel was considered. You will recall that there is a natural side channel in this area. However, because the Pallid Sturgeon has no natural instinct to seek an alternative path, the bypass channel "exit" from the main stem of the river needed to be enhanced in a location where the Pallid Sturgeon would likely encounter it as a reasonable path forward. However, it was assumed that even with an enhanced exit, many of the Pallid Sturgeon would miss the bypass channel and still not be able to negotiate the height of the dam. The rock ramp was considered the better alternative in terms of both likely success and overall costs (Jordon 2013).

Regardless of the method for getting Pallid Sturgeon upstream from the diversion dam, once they were above the dam, they would have faced the added peril of possible entrainment through the irrigation headgate and into the main canal. This entrainment issue led some farmers in the area to be concerned that their entire irrigation system was at risk:

> There's a push to get rid of the Intake dam, which is not really a dam, it slows the water down so it can come in the canal. Well, they're wanting to do away with that, and that would be impossible because those farmers can't afford to pay for a pumping project. (Farmer near Intake 2006)

The farmers worried that the entire irrigation facility would be shut down in favor of a truly free-flowing river. A joint effort by the Bureau of Reclamation and the Army COE, completed in 2012, alleviated most of those concerns. Officials decided to address the entrainment issues first by installing a new headgate that provides irrigation water that is equipped with screens to keep the fish out of the canal. The new structure is just upstream from the older headgate (Figure 3.3).

Figure 3.3 New headgates at Intake

Photo: Bureau of Reclamation

Unfortunately, in 2013, the rock ramp alternative was deemed not feasible (U.S. Bureau of Reclamation 2018). The problem was that only approved materials could be placed in the river (i.e., blocks of granite), and these materials were much more expensive than anticipated. When potential contractors submitted bids for the project, their figures were consistently twice the amount estimated by design engineers. The rock ramp was no longer financially feasible, and managers returned to the notion of the enhanced bypass channel. Because of the change in plans, the next seven years were punctuated by lawsuits, injunctions, reevaluations, and revised planning. Each turn in the story was reported in local newspapers. A complete account of the fits and starts will not be fully discussed here. Instead, a few of the important junctures are outlined as follows.

By 2016, a new analysis was prepared that, again, considered the alternative courses of action. At this juncture, it was estimated that the rock ramp would cost nearly $60 million. In comparison, the bypass alternative would cost approximately $50 million. As such, the rock ramp was no longer the first choice (U.S. Bureau of Reclamation 2016). The managing agencies argued that the bypass project should be approved, and they opened a new bidding process. The associated costs of the new plan surprised community members. One McKenzie County, North Dakota farmer described it as, "ridiculous … with the amount they're talking, you could give each [Pallid] a limousine ride up there every day for a long time" (2006). Then, before the bypass decision was finalized, legal injunctions to stop the bypass project were filed by the advocacy group Defenders of Wildlife (Brown 2015). This group's primary purpose is to "prevent species and their habitats from becoming imperiled" (Defenders of Wildlife 2020). The suit argued that the bypass would not solve the problem because most fish would continue to miss the exit from the main channel. The injunctions were upheld, but the COE appealed the decision.

In April 2018, the 9th Circuit Court ruled that the lower court had erred in issuing the injunction (Jean 2018). The Circuit Court had cleared the way for the project to start, but the construction contracts had already been canceled, forcing authorities to conduct new environmental and cost analyses before announcing a new bidding process. Later in 2018, the project was announced, this time to include the bypass channel and a new replacement weir (diversion dam). By this time local farmers seemed mostly satisfied that, although it is an expensive solution, the new Intake headgate would work for irrigation. People had come together for a common cause:

> About the Pallid Sturgeon and the Intake thing, most people are all on the positive side. "Let's get this thing done. Let's help out the fish and help out the farmers. Water for the fish, and water for the farmers." … But they put in these expensive fish screens and … these screens get all the mud and whatnot. They have to lift them out every so often and hose the mud off of them because the Yellowstone is really a muddy river. It has all kinds of debris in it, too. So anyway, they spend a lot of money on those fish screens, to keep the fish out of the canal. (Farmer near Sidney 2018)

Another farmer explained that even though he had lingering concerns about the motives of advocacy groups, he was satisfied with the bypass channel:

> I still don't think they're going to be happy until the dam, or the weir, is gone. But I think the fish bypass will work. It's proven that it works over in France. I don't know why it wouldn't work here. Heck, it gives the fish more surface to go swim, more area.

> You know, I think it's a good idea, and it serves both purposes. It would keep the fish happy, and it would keep us happy. (Farmer near Sidney 2018)

Yet another twist occurred in January 2019. As soon as the latest bidding process was completed, a losing bidder challenged the contract, forcing another delay (Stuart 2019). Within a few months, that challenge was dismissed by the court. In July 2019, the work at Intake was finally underway (Herbaugh 2019).

We can think about the ESA as an environmental sustainability agenda, one designed to recover a species to the extent that their long-term well-being is no longer in doubt. Unfortunately, in the case of the Pallid Sturgeon, the end goal is still very remote. Even if the bypass channel and the new headgates work as desired, it seems unlikely that the species can survive without continuing human intervention in the reproductive processes of the Pallid Sturgeon: "As for their sustainability, it doesn't seem possible without the hatcheries" (Michael Backes, e-mail message to Susan Gilbertz, July 06, 2020).

Long-Term Sustainability of the Cottonwood Forests

As a second example of environmental sustainability in the Yellowstone River Valley, we will next examine the health and well-being of the cottonwood forests. These forests are important to the local landscape. They send off millions of cotton-tufted seeds in the spring, they are colorful harbingers of autumn, and they provide habitat for many species of birds, some rare and some common. As a personal anecdote, when one author participated in a winter canoe float near Billings, she witnessed 12 pairs of Bald Eagles living in cottonwood trees in the space of only about five river miles. These eagles were easy to spot because the foliage was off the trees, and some were fishing the river as her canoe passed. Throughout the Yellowstone River Valley, locals and visitors are struck by the beauty of these forests and by the avian communities that depend on them for habitat.

It is easy to find old growth cottonwood forests near the Yellowstone River (Figure 3.4). Local residents throughout the Yellowstone River Valley appreciate the cottonwoods as giants of arboreal magnificence, and many landowners can prove that individual cottonwood trees have survived on their properties for well over 100 years (Gilbertz, Horton, and Hall 2006). They refer to historical photographs of family picnics and weddings held in the shady areas down near the river. Often, the cottonwood trees in their backyards are living legacies of the efforts and toils of great-grandparents who wanted to leave the immediate environment in better condition for their progeny. One retiree, who moved from Billings to live outside of town and on the riverbank, explained the affections of his wife and himself, "We love cottonwood trees ... Picture this place without a cottonwood or with no trees, it would be the Sahara Desert. We love the trees" (Riverbank Retiree near Grey Cliff 2018).

Figure 3.4 Cottonwood Forest in Fall

The plains cottonwood (*Populus deltoides*, subspecies *monilifera)* is prevalent in the lower Yellowstone River Valley (Dixon et al. 2012), and the narrowleaf (*Populus angustifolia*) is the dominant cottonwood in the upper valley near Gardner (see Merigliano, Friedman, and Scott 2013). Individual cottonwood trees will not reach seed-bearing age until their 10th year, and they will not reach full development until they are 40 or 50 years old (Cooper and Van Haverbeke 1990). They require good sunlight; thus, invasive trees and shrubs can negatively affect the success of juvenile cottonwood trees if the invasive trees create too much shade. However, under favorable conditions, many cottonwoods will easily live over 90 years, and the oldest known trees have survived for over 300 years

(Friedman and Griffin 2017). Specific to the Yellowstone River basin, research shows that some cottonwood trees in the Powder River and the lower Yellowstone River drainages are over 270 years old (Schook, Friedman, and Rathburn 2016).

Cottonwoods are considered "thirsty" and many stands are aged. They need to tap into reliable groundwater to survive (Scott, Auble, and Friedman 1997). Therefore, they tend to do well on river and streambanks (Lesica 2012). However, in some regions and watersheds, cottonwood forests are made up of mostly mature trees (Braatne et al. 2007). Across Montana, including many areas of the Yellowstone River Valley, there is an apparent lack of young cottonwood trees, and an "aging out" of the forests has been noted for at least two decades (Auble and Scott 1998; Dixon et al. 2012; Johnson et al. 2012). In 2013, in the upper river near Gardiner, researchers found a "scarcity of trees less than about 100 years old" (Merigliano, Friedman, and Scott 2013, 161).

A study of avian species in the Yellowstone River Valley by Jones (2014) offers direct and indirect evidence of forest decline. For ecologists, select species can serve as indicator species, which means that patterns of their presence or absence can be interpreted as a measure of overall richness (i.e., number of species) and completeness of a larger suite of organisms (i.e., biotic community; Fleishman et al. 2005). In this way, indicator species serve to help assess the overall health of an ecosystem. Because some groups of birds have similar habitat and resource requirements, those species will collectively avoid areas where the habitat is no longer suitable. As such, the absence (or near absence) of certain avian species (bald eagles, osprey) along the Yellowstone River has been interpreted as a measure of decline in health of the cottonwood forests. Jones (2014) was able to demonstrate distinct patterns of bird abundance and absence. She also noted forest conditions, and her work helped verify a trend that had been observed for some time. Namely, in many areas it was difficult to find new cottonwood recruits, either as seedlings or as stands of juvenile trees. As indicator species, the avian communities of the Yellowstone River function a bit like canaries in coal mines because they alert us to potential problems.

Our interviews confirmed that, out of love, or out of worry, people have noticed the advanced age of the cottonwood forests throughout the

Yellowstone River Valley. One resident said, "They've been there as long as we can remember" (Riverbank Residents near Columbus 2018). Another commented, "We've got a lot of old cottonwoods up and down Main Street. Oh my God, they're just beautiful, magnificent trees, but some of them are starting to die … God, I hate to see those majestic old trees go" (City Official in Big Timber 2018). In Livingston, a homeowner with a view of the riverbank said, "There's a lot of cottonwoods, but they're dying out. They're old" (Local Historian in Livingston 2018). Others were aware of the aging and regeneration processes they have witnessed. One explained the importance of high water in the spring, locally referred to as the "June Rise":

> I mean you've got hundred-year-old trees … After the June Rise, that silt brings those cottonwood seeds. They'll start, and they'll grow three feet that first year. For three years they'll be so thick you can't walk through them. Then they start to die out and thin out as they get bigger and more mature. It's incredible how fast they'll grow. (Avid Hunter near Miles City 2018)

One resident suggested he might even see a connection between the lack of new cottonwoods and abundance of Russian olive trees, which, along with salt cedar, are now considered invasive along the Yellowstone River corridor (Kellogg 2016):

> There's an awful lot of big ones, you know. There are places where you see them, but they're not coming back like gangbusters. Russian olives are thick, of course. But you know when I was a kid there were no Russian olives in this country." (Avid Boater near Sheppard 2018)

Some residents are more explicit in their theories regarding the aging and decline of cottonwoods. They note that high water in the spring can erode the riverbank, "Cottonwoods have fallen during high flood water, you know. They get pulled in" (Avid Fisher near Livingston 2018). A resident in Glendive explained that because he sees old forests, and because he knew that grazing and farming practices were all having negative impacts on cottonwood regeneration, he was allowing spaces in some fields for cottonwood trees to grow:

> Your hundred-year-old cottonwoods start getting old, and there's no new growth ... The sad part is, if you're grazing, then the cows will keep those cottonwoods out because they love cottonwoods ... They are one of the first things the cows will eat. And they'll eat them down to nothing. And there's no recruitment in the forest areas where you already have big cottonwoods ... On one parcel, where we had been planting barley, it flooded in 2011 ... [Once the flooding receded] we had thousands of little cottonwood seedlings. So, I didn't farm it. I waited. After five years, I went back and tilled the field again, but we left three big patches of cottonwoods. It's pretty cool. It's been about eight years, and the cottonwoods are about ten feet tall now. (Farmer Overlooking the River at Glendive 2018)

Interestingly, approximately 20 miles east of Billings, at Pompey's Pillar National Monument, early drawings and photographs of the area suggest many fewer cottonwood trees at the site than are found today. The site was a camp for Captain Clark and his men in 1806, and early documentation of the area is spotty. However, it is speculated that in the same way cattle will happily graze on cottonwood seedlings, in the early 1800s, migrating bison might have eaten the majority of seedlings each spring.

Over the past 20 years, concerted efforts have gone into understanding the reproductive mechanisms of the cottonwoods, and much more is now known (Borman and Larson 2002; Friedman and Griffin 2017; Merigliano, Friedman, and Scott 2013; Nielsen et al. 2010; Schook, Friedman, and Rathburn 2016). To begin, cottonwoods are prolific producers of seed, and seed production remains undeterred. The seeds are tiny, and their accompanying "cotton" means they are easily transported by the wind or on the surface of moving water. However, the seeds are viable for only a short period of time, meaning there is a narrow window of time, referred to as the "recruitment box," for a seed to become a seedling. Mahoney and Rood (1998) modeled recruitment as a function of the timing of flows relative to when seeds are being produced and released.

The model demonstrates specific conditions for cottonwood seeds to take root.

According to the USGS, cottonwood seeds need "bare, moist sites," typically caused when spring flows cause channel changes, meandering, and shifting depositions of materials (Auble et al. 2005). In other words, the seeds do best when they find exposed muddy banks or bars. While extended flooding can depress growth, successful recruitment of seedlings is nonetheless dependent on temporary flood inundations (Amlin and Rood 2001). Where there is no flood inundation, there will not be seedlings; where the inundations last too long, the seeds will not survive.

There are several mechanisms that can be involved in recruitment (Scott, Auble, and Friedman 1997), and sandbars provide an apt illustration of how cottonwood recruitment can work. The high river flows of spring are likely to move materials, such as silts, sands, and gravels, which are then deposited to new locations, perhaps on a point bar on the inside of a river bend. As the flows recede, a new bare and moist area is exposed that is perfect for seedling recruitment. A sandbar might begin as a small area, but it can grow with each flood season if the area is repeatedly inundated with water that deposits more sand and gravel. Each year, after the floods, the sandbar has new surface for cottonwood recruitment. The sandbar can host a new generation of recruits each spring, and the overall effect is this: on the edges and near the tip of the sandbar, the trees are just saplings. Further back, the trees are juveniles. And yet further back, the stand is increasingly more mature. In this scenario, the overall forest never ages out because several generations of cottonwoods are growing near one another. We know that the successful recruitment of young cottonwood trees is greatly dependent on channel migrations and flood regimes that produce these excellent recruitment sites.

Moreover, there is little wonder as to why the lower Yellowstone River Valley has fewer and fewer young cottonwood recruits on its banks. The flood regime of the valley has undergone significant changes, and the greatest changes are associated with the Big Horn River. About 50 miles east of Billings, the Big Horn River enters the Yellowstone River as a primary tributary to the lower river (see border of Reaches B12 and C1). Historically, its tremendous spring flows caused downstream flooding, but once the June Rise had passed, the river levels dropped and flooding receded. By mid-summer, the river had low flows. This pattern of wet-then-dry persisted year after year, and the annual mechanics of flooding and sediment transport created favorable conditions for cottonwood regeneration. However, these cycles did not continue unchanged.

In 1944, the Pick–Sloan Flood Control Act (P.L. 78-534) was approved by Congress (U.S. Bureau of Reclamation n.d.b). The act was designed to help minimize flood risks, generate hydropower, provide irrigation water in late summer, and, especially, ensure continuous barge navigation on the Missouri River (Schneiders 1999). It is estimated that between 1950 and 1999, the Pick–Sloan Missouri Basin Program provided over two billion dollars in flood control benefits (Pick Sloan n.d.). Both Wyoming and Montana lobbied for construction of Yellowtail Dam, which would use the Big Horn Canyon in Wyoming to create a reservoir on the Big Horn River. The Yellowtail Dam project was completed in the 1960s, and it included recreational opportunities at the Big Horn Canyon National Recreation Area (U.S. National Park Service 2015). It was one of the last large dams built by the federal government.

The communities of the lower Yellowstone River Valley benefitted greatly from Yellowtail Dam. This area was once heavily and frequently inundated with flood waters; however, Yellowtail Dam changed the flood regime. While Yellowtail Dam did not fully eliminate the possibility of downstream spring floods, people living in towns such as Forsyth, Miles City, and Glendive could assume that the dangers of such floods were much reduced, and they could count on having water in the hottest months of summer. Today, downstream from the confluence of the Big Horn and Yellowstone Rivers, one finds a resulting shift in land use as compared to the 1950s. In some areas (e.g., Reach C9), what once served as floodplains have been converted to developed agricultural lands. Because of both increased agricultural development and the construction of the dam, it has been noted that "the main alterations to the hydrology of the Yellowstone River are due to irrigation and flood control" (CEA 2015, 127).

Installation of the dam not only changed the spatial extent of flooding, it altered the timing and amounts of flows over annual periods. Analyses show that had there been no water development from 1928 until 2002, the

June Rise at a gaging station just downstream from the confluence of the Big Horn River would have averaged 14,600 cubic feet per second (cfs), August flows would have averaged 5,610 cfs, and January flows would have dwindled to 1,970 cfs (Chase 2014, 79; Figure 3.5). Comparatively, had the 2002 level of water development been in place during the entire period, the June flows would have averaged 6,600 cfs, August flows would have averaged 2,830 cfs, and January flows would have averaged 3,120 cfs. With Yellowtail Dam and other water development infrastructure in place, the overall pattern is a leveling of the flow, and gone are the days of wet-then-dry floodplains. It is easy to see, then, how cottonwood recruitment, which depends on periodic wet and dry periods, would be affected by the dam's stabilizing effect on river flows.

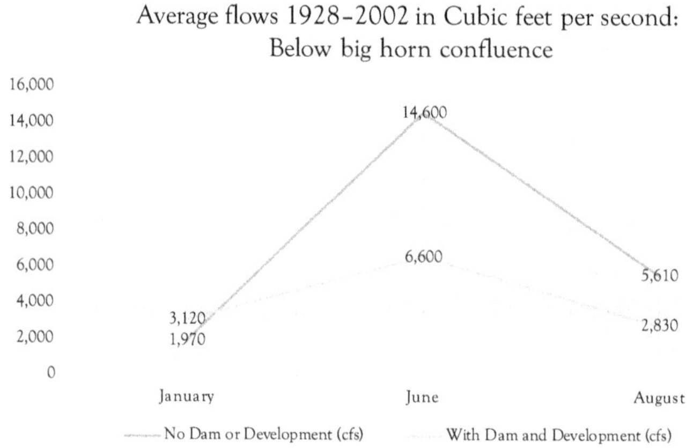

Figure 3.5 Comparing flows: With and without dam and development

It is also worth considering that the flood regime may have shifted because of climate change and that such changes may also directly and indirectly affect cottonwood recruitment. Some people in the valley claim that the June Rise is now most likely to occur in May. In fact, when comparing recent data to information gathered in the mid-20th century, in some locations the timing of spring flows is clearly in flux (U.S. Geological Survey 2005). In the upper Yellowstone River Valley, state officials predict three consequences of climate change: (1) earlier runoff, (2) faster runoff, and (3) diminished late-season flow (Dalby 2018). If seed production, pollination, and flooding are out of sequence, cottonwood recruitment is less likely. Field evidence from the upper basin near Gardiner and Livingston led modelers to conclude that the "small areas of forest established in the last 75–100 years suggested a decrease in river activity caused, at least in part, by a climate-induced decrease in peak flows" (Merigliano, Friedman, and Scott 2013, 162).

Despite the leveling effects of the dam, the Yellowstone River remains fairly flood dynamic as compared with other rivers. As recently as 2011 and 2017, many areas in the lower river flooded. Yet, there is little doubt that climate change and 60-some years of flood management in the lower valley has had an impact on the long-term well-being of the cottonwood forests. Using tree rings as evidence, researchers have compared the health of trees during the 1800s to the well-being of trees today:

> The flow reconstructions revealed droughts and wet periods in the 1800s more extreme than any occurring in the historical record. Declines in growth at the Yellowstone and Powder Rivers beginning in the mid-to-late 1900s resulted partly from flow regulation, which delayed much of the runoff until after the early-summer period when most tree ring growth occurs. (Schook, Friedman, and Rathburn 2016, 1870)

In Chapter 1, we noted that it takes much work to understand the myriad factors and changes that might shift our calculations when attempting to manage forests for harvest. Similarly, we must continue to investigate a variety of questions, and to creatively explore ecologically grounded ideas, if we intend to address the long-term well-being of cottonwood forests. For instance, one study investigated whether changing flood and drought regimes created spatial problems in cottonwood regeneration (Nielsen et al. 2010). If male and female cottonwood trees had different tolerances to variation in water availability, the researchers reasoned, it was possible that spatial separations might emerge that would subsequently prevent seed germination. However, evidence of spatial segregations was not strong, and more recent evidence shows that among the oldest of cottonwood trees, male and female trees survive equally well (Friedman and

Griffin 2017, 12, Figure 11). Thus, even though our investigations do not always prove our hypotheses, such studies are important. They are examples of the types of questions we will need to investigate as we endeavor to understand, and perhaps help ensure, the long-term well-being of the cottonwood forests.

It seems fair to question whether our current practices, left unchanged, will result in long-term environmental sustainability of the valley. The examples of the endangered Pallid Sturgeon and declining cottonwood forests illustrate that the impacts of human activities, including climate change, are linked to sustainability problems. The examples also illustrate that economic and environmental sustainability interests cannot be addressed in isolation from one another, and that any one remedy is unlikely to be wholly satisfactory. The ESA of 1973 functions to help ensure a more sustainable environment for certain species, but not without controversy and certainly not necessarily quickly. The Pallid Sturgeon was listed as an endangered species in 1990. Thirty years later, we are finally on the cusp of remediating one of the biggest obstacles to the long-term well-being of the Pallid Sturgeon, the blockage at Intake. As for cottonwood regeneration, it is unlikely that we will choose to remove Yellowtail Dam, and, thus, complete remedies are difficult to imagine. At the very least, we could work toward understanding flooding as an important natural process that we can value in terms of its positive consequences. Moreover, it may be that efforts to address dwindling Pallid Sturgeon populations and cottonwood forests can be linked. Perhaps, that which is good for the Pallid Sturgeon might also be good for the cottonwood trees. It will take creative thinkers to imagine how to address these issues, and it will require the engagement of many.

Discussion Questions

We might begin by pondering the long-term well-being of the Pallid Sturgeon:

1. In what ways does the Endangered Species Act of 1973 represent efforts of a previous generation to address long-term environmental sustainability for us?

2. Will the bypass channel, the alternative that was initially considered flawed, be adequate? How will we know? What if it does not work?
3. Should we continue to fund our federal and state hatcheries as a means of insuring the well-being of the Pallid Sturgeon as a species? Is this a sustainable approach?
4. What are some of the current factors, especially ones not thought of in 1990, that will affect whether the Pallid Sturgeon are sustained?

Assuming we care about cottonwood forests, we should think about these questions:

1. Do we need further scientific proof of the aging of the cottonwood forests along the Yellowstone River corridor? What kind of further data might be helpful?
2. If a sustained cottonwood population largely relies on conserving dynamic river processes, how might we ensure those processes?
3. If some of the factors leading to the decline of the cottonwood forests are global in scale, what might Montanans do locally?

How do residents' comments concerning Pallid Sturgeon and cottonwood forests illustrate sensitivity to sustainability's central question? If dozens of farmers leave "big patches of cottonwoods" or purposefully "plant wildflowers" near their fields, how many patches would it take to make a difference?

Easy Access Resources

Bureau of Reclamation, Record of Decision, 2016: www.usbr.gov/newsroom/newsroomold/newsrelease/detail.cfm?RecordID=57556

Endangered Species Act https:www.fws.gov/international/laws-treaties-agreements/us-conservation-laws/endangered-species-act.html

National Fish Hatchery at Garrison Dam: www.fws.gov/mountain-prairie/fisheries/garrisonDam_pdfs/Garrison%20Dam%20NFH_Pallid SturgeonRecovery.pdf

Pick–Sloan Missouri Basin Program: www.usbr.gov/projects/index.php?id=380

U.S. Army Corps of Engineers, Missouri Recovery Plan: www.nwo.usace.army.mil/mrrp/efforts-actions/YS-Intake/

U.S. Fish and Wildlife, Revised Recovery Plan, 2014: www.pallidSturgeon.org/wp-content/uploads/2012/11/Pallid-Sturgeon-Recovery-Plan-First-Revision-signed-version-012914_3.pdf

Yellowstone River Cumulative Effects Analysis: http://ftp.geoinfo.msl.mt.gov/Documents/Projects/Yellowstone_River_Clearinghouse/Yellowstone-River-Cumulative-Effects-Study.pdf

CHAPTER 4

Social Well-Being in the Yellowstone River Valley

Introduction

Our third component of sustainability, social sustainability, occurs when communities engage in "life-enhancing" practices (McKenzie 2004). Moreover, when a society provides opportunities for its members to improve their well-being, social sustainability requires that society must also ensure that the opportunities are managed fairly. As you can imagine, social sustainability questions are far-reaching, including topics such as upward mobility and access to quality education. Recent analyses evaluate factors such as personal security, individual freedom, the rule of law, and trust in government (Legatum Institute 2019). These studies disclose patterns of geographical inequalities—global, national, and within Montana—that will apply to our case study of the Yellowstone River Valley. To achieve social sustainability, we must recognize when some people are disenfranchised from opportunities because of social inequities, and we must find ways to correct those situations.

Correcting inequities must include addressing our practices, whether they be habits or codified rules. Even when we do not intend to do so, our practices can generate, propagate, and institutionalize unfair outcomes, such as racism, sexism, and classism. Social sustainability asks us to examine how well our traditions, customs, rules, and laws result in fairness and justice. We should willingly evaluate our processes and procedures, and when they are shown to be unfair, we must either institute new rules and practices or reform old ones. Sometimes, old ways of doing things hamper fairness in contemporary circumstances. Sometimes, a lack of rules can be problematic. Future generations will not simply inherit economic and environmental conditions, they will also inherit a set of customs and laws.

We begin by thinking about specific terms relating to social sustainability: fairness, equality, equity, accountability, and environmental justice. Then, we will apply those understandings to concerns in the Yellowstone River Valley. We will make a distinction between private and public resources because in the United States that distinction implicates very different rules of fairness. Also, by examining how mishaps in the oil and gas field are resolved, we begin to ask if we might design our system of practices, rules, and laws to elicit better results. Chapter 4 ends by examining whether social stability is essential to social sustainability. In these examples, it becomes clear that the long-term social well-being of the people of the Yellowstone River Valley is linked to how we manage our industries and natural resources.

Important Terms and Distinctions

Social sustainability asks us to actively practice *fairness* (Eizenberg and Jabareen 2017). Sometimes, fairness in a situation causes us to expect *equality*, whereby all parties have the same rights and opportunities. Consider the situation of two siblings, each receiving a weekly monetary allowance for performing household chores. In a system of perfect equality, the tasks assigned to each sibling are equal and the paid allowances are equal. However, circumstances are seldom so perfect, and families often turn to *equitable* formulas to achieve fairness. Equity is achieved when an agreed-upon principle defines fairness (Deutsch 1975). For instance, an equitable formula concerning the siblings might increase one sibling's weekly earnings to recognize extra efforts. Likewise, when the parents decide to arrange their estate, they might decide to treat each child equally, or equitably. In a situation where one child has serious health concerns and one does not, the parents might decide that the child with continuing medical expenses should receive a larger share of the estate. They equitably provide for the futures of both children by giving the unhealthy child a larger share. Fairness, then, does not always take the form of equality. Rather, the principle of equity is considered fair when there is a rationale for determining unequal outcomes.

Our customs and laws can sometimes help families striving to operate fairly. For example, some parents will adhere to a long-standing principle of rural life, *primogeniture*, when arranging their estate: the family's landholdings will go to the oldest male child (Bertocchi 2006). This practice is viewed as a necessity when farms are too small to be economically viable if the landholdings are divided, and, therefore, the estate must seemingly be given to only one child. Moreover, because estate laws allow for unequal divisions, the tradition has been codified.

In terms of fairness, *accountability* is also a factor in social well-being. For instance, when two automobile drivers are involved in an accident, it seems fair that the person who caused the accident should pay for the repairs. Even when the mishap is truly an accident, we expect responsible parties to be held accountable. By the 1990s, fairness and accountability were being widely discussed in terms of environmental justice (Adamson et al. 2002). It had become obvious that many of our industrial practices resulted in situations where environmental costs were incurred by persons far removed from the benefits being reaped. For example, most people who wear blue jeans are never confronted with the environmental impacts of the dyes and acids used in the manufacturing processes. Economists use the term *negative externalities* to refer to costs incurred by third parties who are not engaged in a transaction but who are forced to absorb negative consequences (Cornes and Sandler 1986).

When our practices allow the consequential environmental degradations from an economic transaction to occur elsewhere, or when the impacts of the degradations are not included in the costs to the consumers, we engage an environmental injustice. By subscribing to a philosophy of *environmental justice*, we are asked to not ignore situations where others absorb the negative environmental consequences of our practices and consumptive desires.

The EPA explains environmental justice as, "the fair treatment and meaningful involvement of all people regardless of race, color, national origin, or income, with respect to the development, implementation, and enforcement of environmental laws, regulations, and policies" (U.S. Environmental Protection Agency 2020). In other words, when it comes to our environment, justice means our rules must be designed and implemented to achieve fairness. We must be willing to change rules that disproportionately harm some people while benefiting others who do not incur all of the consequential costs.

As social beings, we practice customs, and we invent rules and laws to help us understand and achieve fairness. These practices and inventions help with mundane issues (calculating weekly allowances), with personal legacies (estates), with assigning responsibilities (settlements), and with guarding against unfair consequences (justice). Each of the following examples should help bring into focus concerns about fairness and social well-being that deserve our attention.

Examples of Fairness in Public Resources

Issues of fairness can involve natural resources, some of which are held publicly and some privately. The United States, with its legal traditions traceable to the laws of Medieval England, derives distinctions regarding public and private resources from the *Magna Carta of Libertatum* of 1215—the Great Charter of Liberties. Among other legal concerns, this document laid a foundation for modern laws concerning public access to fish and wildlife (Murphy 1968). Yet, these public resources often intersect with private rights. Wildlife often moves across private lands, and, in the case of fish, their streams may run through private properties.

As public resources, fish and wildlife resources are managed by state and federal governmental agencies, and these agencies must mediate the public–private interfaces. The states enact laws to define how hunting and fishing will be practiced within their borders. Typically, these laws include regulations concerning licenses, harvest limits, and seasons, to name a few. The federal government reviews the states' laws to determine if the interests of the public of the larger United States are being addressed. Because wildlife and fish do not recognize state boundaries, larger public interests are assured across state boundaries via federal oversight. For instance, wolves were reintroduced into YNP in 1995 and are now found in Montana, Idaho, Wyoming, Colorado, Oregon, and Washington. Each of these states was required to develop wolf management plans, especially in terms of allowable killing and hunting. The federal government intervened when Wyoming's management plan was deemed inadequate in terms of broader public interests (Jones 2008).

Sometimes, society demands that our laws evolve to offer greater specificity, and many public and private interests have been sorted out statutorily. That is, legislatures have enacted laws that define the boundaries and rights associated with specific public–private interfaces. For instance, in 1985, Montana enacted the Stream Access Law. It clarified that "all surface waters that are capable of recreational use may be so used by the public without regard to the ownership of the land underlying the waters" (Montana Code Annotated § 23-2-302 1985). The public can use the rivers and streams, even if they run across private properties (Figure 4.1). Among many additional provisions and subsections of the law, two are especially important: (1) without permission, the public is not allowed to cross private property to access a waterway, and (2) in every location along the streambank, public access is limited to the "high water mark." A recreational user who fails to respect these rules is engaged in trespass.

Figure 4.1 Fishing the Yellowstone River in Eastern Montana

Yet, there are many situations where laws are not available or where they do not explicitly define rights. In these cases, the courts can be asked to sort out the public and private interests. Some decisions will be based on common law—interpretations of customs or of judicial precedent. In the case of Montana's streams, were a landowner to claim that birdwatching is not true recreation and, thus, commence an argument about trespass with a birdwatcher standing on a riverbank, the courts would assuredly rule in favor of the birder. While birdwatching is not explicitly identified as a recreational use in Montana law, custom demands it be recognized as a long-standing tradition of outdoors enthusiasts.

Importantly, in Montana, hunting and fishing are considered mainstays of recreation. In the parlance of social sustainability, they are considered "life enhancing" activities. However, access issues can make it difficult for the public to exercise their rights to these recreational pastimes. Traditionally, landowners readily granted access to rivers and streams and hunting areas on their properties, but today, some landowners legally block public access:

> I can think of a situation where a guy bought a place specifically for fishing, and he bought a couple miles of [riverbank]. But the guy on the other side of the river was letting whoever wanted to come and go fishing. [The new landowner] didn't like that, so he got a buddy to help him buy the land on the other riverbank. So, now you can't access the river from either side. A lot of that's happening. (Recreational Fisher near Big Timber 2006)

As a larger fairness issue, it does the public little good to know it has recreational rights if there are too few points of access for exercising those rights.

Some advocacy groups have formed in Montana to address issues involving access to public resources. The Public Land/Water Access Association (PLWA) was formed "to maintain, restore, and perpetuate public access to the boundaries of all Montana public land and waters" (Public Land/Water n.d.). Similarly, Our Montana promotes stewardship and the "enjoyment of Montana's natural, historic, and recreational resources" (Our Montana n.d.). More recently, the Lower Yellowstone River Coalition formed to:

> Help expand sustainable outdoor recreation opportunities along the Lower Yellowstone River. We envision a future for eastern Montana where more families want to raise their children here, more small businesses want to set down roots here, and more visitors want to stay and explore. (Lower Yellowstone River Coalition 2021)

Each of these groups is engaged, to varying degrees, in protecting the public's interests. In 2006, an active member of Our Montana explained:

> We are trying to work on the recreation and the access end of things. We had a meeting last week with the DNRC, the Fish Wildlife and Parks, the BLM, and the Bureau of Reclamation, with the idea of a cooperative project trying to bring the private sector in somehow on improving the recreational opportunities on the Yellowstone. It's a huge recreational resource. But if you're going to float the length of it, and you don't know where it's legal to stop to get re-supplied or to have people meet you, you can get into a mess. There needs to be maps. (River Access Activist from Billings 2006).

By 2018, he was able to report some success:

> Our Montana has developed a website called "1001 Things That You Can Do on the Yellowstone River." It's a recreation app. And in that app, we show all the fishing access sites and all of the public land along the Yellowstone River. And, we're showing all the museums along the way and all of the known historical sites. (River Access Activist from Billings 2018)

Some groups work to further enhance access to public resources by obtaining lands and making them available to the public. One such group, operating out of Billings, is the Yellowstone River Parks Association (YRPA). This group has been instrumental in raising private funds to purchase lands along the riverbank for the express purpose of dedicating those lands as public spaces, and it recently helped establish a new public boat launch at Billings. The members envision a series of public parks that will follow the Yellowstone River as a "string of pearls"—parks of varying sizes and purposes, connected by public trails for dozens, or even hundreds, of miles:

> When we started, our vision for the first 500 years of YRPA was to establish a trail on one side of the Yellowstone River from Gardiner … to Fort Union [in North Dakota]. And in the next 500 years, to go back and do the other side. And then, in the next 1000 years, to do all the tributaries, so that there would be trails throughout the watershed. Now that vision might be a bit much for one lifetime; but nevertheless, that was our vision when we started. (YRPA Founding Member 2018)

There is no doubt that the efforts of these nongovernmental organizations make a difference in helping the public avail itself of public resources, but it is notable that fairness is somewhat slippery when considering the public–private (private–public?) interfaces. As public pressures on resources increase, some groups form to safeguard private and specific stakeholder groups' interests, and many groups clearly have local economies in view (see Lower Yellowstone River Coalition 2021). On a different front, the Yellowstone River Conservation District Council formed in 1999 to ensure local participation while the CEA was underway. This group is also focused on voluntary acceptance of shifting managerial priorities. It was their philosophy, from the beginning, that governmental oversight should not expand. The group continues, today, and has engaged two follow-up working groups: one to address invasive woody plants in the river corridor and one to address issues involving irrigation outtakes (Yellowstone River Conservation Districts Council n.d.a). In the upper valley, a coalition of residents, in partnership with governmental agencies, local businesses, and local stakeholder groups, has formed as the Upper Yellowstone Watershed Group (2016). Its overarching goal is "to enhance watershed health and the regional economy." Such groups can take active roles in gathering and disseminating good data concerning river resources and uses.

Each of the groups mentioned in this section has a role to play in defining fair uses of the river's shared resources. Governmental oversight and management of the resources can be aided or hindered by any one of these groups. Collaborations with local groups and local leaders can be helpful (Gilbertz et al. 2011; Horton et al. 2019), but such involvements do not always result in better-informed or better-formulated policies, nor to fair and equitable access to public resources (Gilbertz et al. 2019; Hall et al. 2015).

Examples of Oil and Gas Mishaps

Despite efforts to collaborate smoothly within public–private interfaces, disputes still arise, and some disputes ultimately end up in the courts. Often the issue under litigation is accountability for damages, and so it is important to note the distinction between civil and criminal concerns. When the courts are asked to settle disputes between private parties, it is a civil case; but, when actions violate laws or cause damage to public interests, they are handled by city, county, state, or federal governments as criminal cases. Thus, if a newly constructed highway bridge fails and results in drivers being injured, the contractor who built the bridge would assuredly face multiple lawsuits, some criminal and some civil. In terms of environmental violations, when private parties face charges brought forth by governmental agencies, they often negotiate settlements rather than publicly face criminal charges. Here, we turn our attention to two examples of mishaps in the Yellowstone River Valley, both of which will help us understand public and private concerns.

Our first example concerns an oil spill in the Yellowstone River in 2011, known locally as the Exxon spill. Eventually, it was determined that the spill occurred because ice had scoured the river bottom to a depth that exposed a "buried" pipeline that crossed under the river. Later—when the river was running fast and high—a large tree that had fallen into the river snagged the pipeline, causing a rupture. The incident occurred near the town of Laurel, just west of Billings (Reach A18). It was estimated that 63,000 gallons of crude oil spilled into the river (Montana Department of Justice 2016). The crude oil affected water quality and the health and habitats of wildlife and fish; thus, the U.S. Department of the Interior and the State of Montana were involved in determining the impacts to public resources.

Several individual property owners were also affected by the spill. For the most part, the landowners were befuddled by what ensued in the wake of the event. They expected help from governmental entities but were left largely on their own to muddle through long and confusing bureaucratic and legal processes. Less than a year after the spill, one impacted landowner described what happened, in these words:

> [My wife] had walked down to the river that morning to see how high [the river] was, and she ran into oil all over the place. She called me and said, "You're not going to believe this. … We've got an oil spill." … She came back to the house and went online right away. Sure enough, we found out there had been a pipeline burst … We could smell it. But … we weren't notified by anybody.
>
> … I tried to contact Exxon … and all I could get was their security guy … He refused to allow me to talk to anybody … I was concerned. Are we in danger? What are we breathing? Do I need to … get my livestock out of there? They wouldn't let me talk to anybody, so I just asked him, "If this was you, what would you do?" And he said, "I don't know." And I said, "Seriously? You work at a refinery and you have no training on what to do if an oil spill happens?" [Eventually,] they gave me an insurance adjustor's number … [but] I didn't want to file a claim. I wanted to know if I was in danger … The oil was moving in big slicks … [and] there were these big sections of tar … maybe twenty by thirty [square feet] … You could see the oil in the cattails … It was everywhere.
>
> … I was really, really, really disappointed in our County … I've heard [one County Commissioner] say that he was out there at seven o'clock [on the day of the spill] … Well, I was talking to him at nine o'clock that morning, and he sure wasn't anywhere near the river … The state [DEQ], in the long run, was very helpful … but that first morning [there was not] much they could do. They were trying to get their heads around the problem.
>
> … It was kind of shocking … You think, okay, go to DEQ, or go to your county officials … The reality was everybody just kept

steering us back to Exxon. Exxon was in charge ... [but] they did not want to tell you anything. All they wanted to do was get the insurance claims filed. And at that point, we have no idea what the damages were. How were we supposed to file an insurance claim? ... You think this is what government is for, but government is just referring you back to the private corporation that caused the problem in the first place, and [the corporation] has an interest in not necessarily telling you everything ... Right away they said it was only seven hundred barrels, and then it moved up to one thousand barrels, and then it moved up to fourteen hundred barrels ... It was ridiculous.

... The EPA was a profound, profound disappointment ... They were using the industry's language, "this was a risk-management operation," [and] they continually talked down to the public ... I remember seeing one flow chart about how the whole cleanup process was going to work ... There were all these boxes and [lines] going everywhere. As an outlier, one box said, "Consult Landowner." It was at the bottom, after the whole flow chart is done.

... Had the State of Montana not stepped up, then we would have had a lot harder time working with the EPA and working with Exxon ... The Governor came in and leaned heavily on EPA to work with landowners ... The State was the only one encouraging people to get out there and document, verify, and get your soils tested.

... We won't know [how the rupture happened] until lawsuits and discovery start happening. It sounds to me like the pipeline had been exposed for some time ... We learned that the other refineries had shut down their pipelines during this [high water] time. So, I think everybody [in the industry] had a reasonable suspicion that something could happen. And I think Exxon weighed their chances and decided it was worth the risk.

... I think part of it also has to do with the fact that we have aging infrastructure. I don't know if there needs to be additional regulatory oversight over the pipeline industry or if we just need to fully reassess how we're moving oil. But, I think we do have a

> problem … We need to realize accidents happen, and we need to be prepared for them. They might only happen once every twenty or thirty years, but when they happen, they have a significant effect. (Riverside Farmer near Laurel 2012)

While the responses of this landowner—to the spill, to expectations about government, and to the inevitability of accidents—were highly personalized, those reactions are not uncommon among residents of the valley around the likelihood and impacts of pipeline ruptures (Emerson, Hall, and Gilbertz 2021). Six years later, the same landowner explained his dissatisfaction with the resolution for him as an impacted private party:

> We ended up having to sue them. They settled. I'm not satisfied with it … They basically ceased all cleanup activities on our place pretty quickly … even though we got more attention because we were a very, very squeaky wheel. When it came down to … the remediation in our bottom pastures, they brought in a mine reclamation crew, not farmers. They … tilled the soil about eighteen to twenty-four inches deep … Nothing grows there anymore … We took twenty-five acres of really nice Yellowstone River bottom soil … and buried it … I imagine we're going to struggle with that all of my life. (Riverside Farmer near Laurel 2018)

It took until 2016 for the State of Montana to arrive at a settlement with Exxon (Montana Department of Justice 2016). As defined in the final document, the damages to public interests included debris piles and negative impacts to terrestrial/riparian habitat, riverine aquatic habitat, American White Pelicans, and recreational uses (State and Federal Trustees 2017). The settlement of $12 million would be variously divided and used to address concerns in each category over the next few years. However, some Montanans questioned the amount of the overall settlement. A watchdog organization reported that in 2012, Exxon held 16 billion dollars in cash reserves (Leber 2012).

In our second example of an oil and gas mishap, we will see that even when some elements of the oil and gas industry are more carefully managed, problems can still be difficult to resolve. As context for this second case, it is important to note that the Montana Board of Oil and Gas Conservation (MBOGC) requires companies to post bonds that create a fund to be used to address problems. The MBOGC understands that the industry is prone to boom-and-bust cycles, and at various junctures some companies will go broke. The bond money can be used by the MBOGC to remediate industrial problems that are left behind when companies go bankrupt or when they move operations out of a location.

Consider the case of gas wells. While they are profitable, production companies regularly attend their maintenance. Yet, when the wells fail to produce enough gas, or when the market drops, some wells are no longer profitable. In these cases, the production companies are supposed to either "shut in" the wells, meaning they use temporary plugs to stop leakage while waiting to see if later conditions suggest the well could (again) be profitable, or they close the wells by permanently plugging them with cement. Unfortunately, if the production company is no longer solvent, wellheads are abandoned—the wellhead is neither shut in, nor is it permanently plugged. One function of the MBOGC is to use money posted as bonds to deal with abandoned leaking wells.

In this example, a gas wellhead located on private land began leaking 10 years after it had been "permanently" plugged. The landowner and the MBOGC were aware that the company had plugged the well and that, 10 years later, the company was still in business and reportedly quite profitable. Noting that the plug had failed, the landowner assumed that the company needed to come back to replug the wellhead. He made numerous calls and wrote several letters to the company's out-of-state headquarters asking them to make the repairs. However, the company refused to take responsibility. Ten years earlier—when the company plugged the well—it had followed the state's requirements, and its work had been inspected by the MBOGC. An attorney told the landowner that because of the inspection, the company was released from further liability.

Once the landowner realized the company would be of no help, he asked the MBOGC to fix the leaking well. The landowner's frustrations grew when at least one official from the MBOGC claimed that bond money was designated for problems with *abandoned* wells. This was not an abandoned well. The landowner remembers being told he should fix the leaking well himself. The landowner, in his late seventies, and having been arguing with company and state officials for over two years, wondered if the leaking well would ever be plugged. On a cold winter day when he and one author visited the wellhead, he noted, "No one is helping me" (Landowner in the Bakken 2013; Figure 4.2).

Figure 4.2 Checking a leaking wellhead in winter

Further inquiries confirmed most of the details of the landowner's story. One difference was that an official at MBOGC claimed the board was trying to get the wellhead fixed, but that the bond fund was too depleted to address the problem immediately. Six months later, it still was not done, and the landowner was still asking the MBOGC for help. One year later, three years after the problem was found, the wellhead was successfully replugged by the MBOGC. Environmentally, the problem was finally resolved.

These examples make us wonder, "Is this the best we can do?" We have devised ways to address problems that involve public resources, but many find the resolutions inadequate. It also seems our rules and laws did little to relieve private parties of inequitable burdens of environmental degradation. We must think carefully about leaving landowners feeling helpless. Well-being should not be built on the misfortunes of even a few individuals. When we allow this, we leave those individuals alienated from their communities (Gilbertz, Anderson, and Adkins 2021).

Social Sustainability and Social Stability

The dynamics of social stability are another important aspect to examine when thinking about social sustainability. Changes to local communities can happen gradually or seemingly overnight, and the communities of the Yellowstone River Valley are sites of both stability and upheaval.

Beyond preservation of local histories, social sustainability also intersects with cultural values and norms. In eastern Montana, where rural sensibilities are still viable, people speak of small-town life as sets of satisfying engagements:

> You know, I've been offered jobs in other towns ... [but] there's just something about living here ... We're so involved in the community. My husband is the Fire Marshal ... I'm an EMT. I'm on the Council. I'm the Assistant Ambulance Coordinator. We're just so involved, community-wise. You know everybody. Everybody cares for everybody else in this community. We always said we're going to leave, but where would we go where we'd be as happy? (First Responder in Eastern Montana 2006)

Yet, these bucolic communities are at risk. Like the cottonwoods, the traditional family farm is also "aging out" (Zentz 2001). Recent statistics from Richland County, Montana, show that among agricultural producers, the average age is over 60 (National Agricultural Statistics Service 2017, 555). Many farms are operated by elders, while younger members of these families leave for opportunities elsewhere. Not only are the "good jobs" of the oil and gas industry not good enough, but the boom-and-bust cycles also disrupt the social fabric of everyday life:

> We really wish the kids would come back. We're four hours away to visit our son, and our daughter lives out on the coast so we get to see her, maybe, twice a year … I just don't think the young people will come back here. There aren't any jobs, there's nothing to do here. Right now, we have an oil thing going on. And, there's all kinds of jobs if you want that work [and lifestyle] … The rig workers came in [from other places] … and were staying in the motels. They were getting off at seven o'clock in the morning, and they'd be going in the bars. They'd be drunk and running around at seven o'clock. (Farmer near Sidney 2006)

It is a complicated task to determine if the boom and the eventual public benefits, such as new fire halls and sewage systems, are fair trades for the social upheavals and subsequent busts experienced by the farm communities of the lower valley. It is even expected that long-term economic, environmental, and social sustainability depend on change, and we might be tempted to argue that it is only fair that the next generation will leave to find good jobs elsewhere. However, it is worth noting the significant population declines in eastern Montana and the potential demise of the local communities (Gloege 2007). For instance, some high schools have fewer than two dozen students, and it is impossible for those school districts to offer a robust slate of courses. One consequence is that students from these districts can be quite disadvantaged if they later choose to enroll in college courses. Communities can choose to consolidate schools across county governments. However, the cost-effectiveness of this type of merger for the government would also result in the loss of local jobs, which for many families provide benefits as well as wages.

In terms of social stability, to argue nostalgically about "the way it used to be" is probably shortsighted, and it may seem simply *unfortunate* for local farmers, on their way to morning coffee, to encounter drunken rig workers. Industries and communities evolve. Sustainable communities must evolve. However, the farmer's lament about his children moving away discloses structural dynamics that put his community at risk. Some of these counties need change. They need industries and communities that offer young people good opportunities.

Because the fabric of every community is interwoven with economic, environmental, and social concerns, it becomes clear that the overall question driving sustainability advocates may be too broad to serve as a call for local action. While we must be willing to ask, "Can we meet our current needs without compromising the ability of future generations to meet their needs," we must also recognize the complexities faced by particular communities. Assuredly, we do not want our habits, customs, rules, or laws to forestall change. Rather, as we attempt to attend to the entire suite of concerns that define our long-term well-being, we need to imagine stability through change.

Discussion Questions

1. In what situations do you expect to be treated as an equal?
2. In what situations are you satisfied with equitable treatment?
3. What are the negative externalities involved in the chapter examples?
4. How is accountability at issue in the chapter examples?
5. How does the rule of law factor into these examples?
6. How might corporate interests differ when the parent company is not based locally, or within the state?
7. How do the chapter examples illustrate intersections of private and public interests?
8. While the rule of law explains that our governments (local, state, and federal) will attend to the public's general interests, in what ways do you also expect those governments to attend to individuals who have been harmed by the actions of others?
9. In the first example, do you accept the settlement as an equitable resolution for lost wildlife habitat, pelicans, and fish?

10. In the second example, do you consider the three years it took to plug the leaking wellhead to be acceptable?
11. Because the private interests were resolved, do the chapter examples illustrate environmental justice?
12. If the efforts of the activist groups (PLWA, Our Montana, and the Yellowstone River Parks Association) help the people of the valley achieve better access to public resources, does that create a more fair society?
13. Need we worry when young people leave an area for opportunities found elsewhere?
14. How can stability be achieved through change?
15. How do the comments made by residents illustrate social sustainability concerns?

Easy Access Resources

Bonding Requirements, as pertaining to Dry and Abandoned Gas Wells in Montana: www.mtrules.org/gateway/RuleNo.asp?RN=36%2E22%2E1308

Environmental Justice: www.epa.gov/environmentaljustice

Montana Board of Oil and Gas Conservation, Online Data: www.bogc.dnrc.mt.gov/WebApps/DataMiner/

Montana's Stream Access Law: https://leg.mt.gov/bills/2017/mca/title_0230/chapter_0020/part_0030/sections_index.html

Our Montana: https://ourmontana.org/about-us/our-mission-and-history/

Public Land/Water Access Association: https://plwa.org/

River Access: "A Big Day for Public Access on the Yellowstone River" (Video): www.youtube.com/watch?v=zRp1YTJ29-8

Settlement of Public Damages, Yellowstone River 2011 Oil Spill: https://media.dojmt.gov/wp-content/uploads/nrdp-yellowstone-restoration.pdf

Yellowstone River 2011 Oil Spill: https://dojmt.gov/lands/yellowstone-river-oil-spill-july-2011/www.theguardian.com/environment/2011/jul/03/yellowstone-river-suffers-oil-spill

Yellowstone River Parks Association: www.yrpa.org/

CHAPTER 5

Sustainability's Complexities

Introduction

As communities face the intersecting nature of sustainability's three primary dimensions, they begin to view change as likely, or even necessary, to their holistic well-being. If they face the threefold challenge as an opportunity to build a vibrant, clean, and fair community, they can do more than address sustainability. They can begin to build resilience.

As defined by Luthar (2006), resilience refers to the ability to make a positive adaptation when faced with a significant adversity. Fleming and Ledogar (2008) note that the word resilience is derived from a Latin term meaning to "jump back up." In other words, resilience refers to the capacity to rebound. The notion was first employed to address an individual's psychological capacity to deal with stress. Later, it was employed to explain the capacity of a community or cultural group to adapt and reorganize itself while retaining key elements that preserve its distinctness (Healy 2006). The concept has also been used for some time by scientists who refer to ecological resilience as "the amount of disturbance that a system can absorb" (Gunderson 2000, 426).

As sustainability scholars, we can employ resilience as a concept that defines our ability to rebound from both foreseeable and unanticipated stressors, especially ones that link our economic, environmental, and social well-being. In this chapter, we will first examine water laws in Montana, which can easily pit individuals against one another. As a matter of resilience, it seems we need to examine our mechanisms for sharing water, especially if we intend to rebound from prolonged and severe droughts. As people and industries call for more water, it may be increasingly difficult for our communities to thrive and developing water-sharing plans before they are needed would enhance our adaptive abilities during a crisis. Later in the chapter, we will examine why our resilience may require us to separately address consumptive and non-consumptive uses of water. Finally, we will examine how the channel migration processes, riparian areas, and floodplains associated with the Yellowstone River are used and adapted. We will see that we are not holistically improving our resilience along the valley floor, even though our long-term well-being depends on our willingness to do so. These examples make clear that resilience must include the intersections of economic, environmental, and social well-being.

Water Is a Shared Resource

Throughout the American west, water is considered a scarce and precious resource. In Montana, the refrain, "Whisky's for drink'n, and water's for fight'n!" rings especially true. Indeed, the first criminal case tried in Montana, *Territory v. Drennan*, was for a shooting involving two irrigators fighting over water (Knowles 1868). Here, we turn our attention to only a few of the many, many details about Montana's water laws and water rights. We will see that fairness in water rights is especially difficult to define because some of the rules reflect priorities set in the 1870s. Efforts to reimagine the rules—even slightly—threaten long-standing cultural assumptions and economic investments. Public and private rights certainly intersect in the context of water laws.

To begin, consider how clearly Montana's constitution lays out the state's unambiguous claim to water as a public resource:

> All surface, underground, fold and atmospheric water within the boundaries of the state are the property of the state for the use of its people and are subject to appropriation for beneficial uses as provided by law. (Constitution of the State of Montana, IX-3)

As property of the state, ownership of water is never transferred away from the state. Rather, water rights can be assigned when the water will be put to a "beneficial use." In Montana, a water-right holder owns only a right to use, and that right is defined in terms of use, amount, and the spatial and temporal limits of the appropriation (Water Policy Interim Committee 2018).

When water is abundant, appropriations can be made to almost anyone for almost any reason. However, in practice, the late summer months present challenges as water is not consistently available for everyone. Many in the valley express concerns about water availability. The Yellowstone Basin Committee, a planning group that convened in 2013, identified as their top two priority concerns: water availability and drought readiness (Gilbertz, Hall, and Ward 2013). As one farmer said, "We need to make people aware that water is a finite material" (Irrigator near Forsyth 2013).

A key concern for rights holders is the clarification of whose rights will supersede when there is not enough water for everyone. When water supplies are inadequate to serve all the rights holders, the prior appropriations doctrine determines who will receive water and who will not (Montana Department of Natural Resources and Conservation 2015b). This doctrine makes it a priority to provide water to the holder who has been using water the longest. In other words, an older appropriation of water will supersede a later appropriation (Water Policy Interim Committee 2018). Understood throughout the American west as "first in time, first in right," the rule prioritizes those with senior rights, and junior rights holders can be forced to stop using water.

Unfortunately, the early bookkeeping regarding legitimate rights and dates of appropriation were messy and easily challenged. In the 1970s, efforts were made to clarify rights as three sets: early rights (essentially guaranteed), rights acquired after implementation of the Montana Water Use Act of 1973 (rights with clear documentation), and the 1978 state-defined water reservations (which defined the rights of eight municipalities, six state and federal agencies, and Conservation Districts with linkages to irrigation projects) (Water Policy Interim Committee 2018). The Montana Water Court, established in 1979, was created to sort out claims and dates of appropriations. It has been busy ever since. Perhaps, then, it was predictable that even in 2013 the basin planning group identified enforcement and protection of senior rights as their third top concern (Gilbertz, Hall, and Ward 2013).

There are two historic bases for Montana's contemporary application of the prior appropriations doctrine. First, the doctrine was confirmed by the Sixth Legislative Assembly of Montana Territory (1870) and was subsequently codified in the Territorial Statutes of 1872. The statute reads, in part, "All controversies respecting the right to water in the territory … shall be determined by dates of appropriation" (see Holloway 1921). This explication, confirmed by the Montana Supreme Court in *Mettler v. Ames Realty Co.* 61 Mont. 152, 201 (1921), protected the White settlers, farmers, and miners who had already arrived and who were already using water.

Second, the doctrine is an underlying principle in the 1872 General Mining Act (GMA), which codifies first mining efforts as priority efforts, meaning whoever first claimed a particular mining location would have the only legal right to develop that location (Squillace 1988). The GMA implicated water rights, too. Given that most mining activities in the late 1800s were conducted via panning or placer techniques, water was needed (Heman 1949). Early miners moved water to the location of their mining claims out of convenience. It was easier to move water to the claim, via canals, sloughs, and sluices, than it was to move the mining materials to the water. Thus, early mining claims and water claims were inherently connected (Bakken 2011).

Some of the early laws and declarations, put in place to protect early White settlers, are mostly still in place today. For instance, in Montana, the application of the beneficial use mandate remains lenient, both in law and in practice. As was true in the 1800s, the state continues to approve wide-ranging uses. Thus, while it is not beneficial to run water downhill simply for the sake of running water, it is beneficial to use water to grow sugar beets, to raise cattle and sheep, to cool oil refineries, to provide water to municipalities, and to run waterslides. Notably, in Montana, no use, or set of uses, is explicitly prioritized over other beneficial uses.

Another concern regarding water rights in Montana is their transferability. A person holding a water right will often transfer that right with land to a buyer or an inheritor. However, the water right can also be severed from the land estate and transferred independently. Water rights can be sold, in and of themselves (Marketing Water Rights n.d.). It is possible that one might own land in Montana where a natural stream runs across the property but not have a right to use the stream's water. The state will formalize the transfer of a water right and its priority date so long as the amount, use, and spatial and temporal delineations of the right remain unchanged. If any of those criteria change, a review must follow to determine if the change will negatively affect other rights holders. In cases where a detrimental impact to other users is expected, the transfer can be denied or the date of appropriation will change to the current date, rather than the historical date. Even though it appears that water has become a commodity, remember the state still holds the water as property. It is the water right that is commodified. In this system of exchange, senior rights are more valuable than junior rights. If one needs water, it is strategic to purchase the oldest right available.

American Indian Water Rights

Montana's water laws have evolved in several ways. In 1908, a famous case was settled by the U.S. Supreme Court in favor of American Indians, establishing their rights to water as Federal Reserved Water Rights. The case, *Winters v. United States* 207 U.S. 564 (1908), involved a conflict on the Fort Belknap Indian Reservation of Montana, home to the A'aninin and the Nakoda nations. The court's decision clarified that, "when the United States sets aside an Indian reservation, it impliedly reserves sufficient water to fulfill the purposes of the reservation, with the priority date established as of the date of the reservation" (U.S. Department of Justice 2015). Throughout the United States, the *Winters* Doctrine established that, at the very least, the minimal water needs of the people living on the reservations must be met.

The limits of water resources were even more of a concern to the people of the Yellowstone River basin in the 1970s because plans to use water for coal development were being widely discussed. Wyoming, Montana, and North Dakota had ratified the Yellowstone River Compact in 1950 (U.S. Geological Survey n.d.c), and the agreement defines how these three states are supposed to share the water supplies of the drainage. Given that both Wyoming and Montana were anxious to develop coal reserves, the compact would, in great measure, determine where such development might occur. Tribal interests were also in play because the tribes were considering developing coal reserves on reservation lands. Importantly, the interstate compact indicates that the states' shares would be "reduced by the shares of water apportioned to the Northern Cheyenne, the Crow, and the Wind River reservation[s]" (Bach 1982).

As a unit of measure, and of water sharing, one must understand "acre-feet," which is a large-scale measure used for water. Specifically, the amount of water needed to cover one acre of land with 12 inches of water is defined as one acre foot. In 1975, the U.S. Department of the Interior projected that by the year 2020, water withdrawals by the Crow and the Northern Cheyenne tribes would total 2.1 million and 500,000 acre-feet per year, respectively (Bach 1982). Tribal rights threatened nontribal water rights holders. One legal scholar explained the situation in 1982 in these terms:

> The reserved rights of the Indians have not been quantified. Under the *Winters* Doctrine, the Indians would have command of the beneficial use of the lands and waters located on the reservation, including necessary uses for the "arts of civilization." This would theoretically include the water necessary for the development of the coal reserves located on the reservations. (Bach 1982, 189)

Indeed, in 1975, the Northern Cheyenne filed a federal suit asking the court to quantify the totality of their water rights (Compact Implementation Program n.d.). Assuming their date of appropriation followed from establishment of their reservation lands, they would have a very senior water right regarding use of water from the Tongue River and Rosebud Creek. As senior rights holders, the tribe would be able to use water in any variety of development projects. Their suit was later dismissed when the U.S. Supreme Court determined that states, not the federal courts, should sort out disputes regarding reserved water rights.

Since then, it is primarily through state adjudications that the full extent of the Indian Reserved Water Rights has been determined—state by state and, typically, tribe by tribe. Because Montana had seven reservations, each with its own claims to water, in 1979 the Montana Legislature created the Reserved Water Rights Compact Commission (RWRCC). The primary task of this commission was to negotiate compacts regarding tribal reserved water rights. In the same sense that states address water disputes via interstate compacts, the commission would negotiate compacts with the tribes that would be used to settle tribal claims to water (Montana Department of Natural Resources and Conservation n.d.).

Each compact would require approval of the Montana Legislature, the U.S. Congress, the tribal community, and the Montana Water Court. Further, even though the states were supposed to negotiate the settlements, in 2019 federal legislation was introduced to provide two billion dollars to settle a tribal claim in the Flathead Basin (U.S. Congress 2019).

Efforts to negotiate the compacts were decades in the making, but the RWRCC generally succeeded in drafting compacts with the tribes of each reservation (Compact Implementation Program n.d.). However, tribal water rights are, to this day, not yet fully resolved as agreements in Montana. In several cases, the processes are incomplete because the approvals are not yet secured. A great deal of state and federal legislative energy has been put into the approval process, but nontribal rights holders, whose claims had previously been senior in definition and whose priority dates are threatened by the confirmation of tribal rights, have asked the legislative bodies to not ratify the compacts (Stern 2019). Ironically, some of the same people who previously staunchly subscribed to the notion of prior appropriations have been threatened by "new" senior rights.

In Montana, the Crow Nations and the Northern Cheyenne now have defined water rights (Compact Implementation Program n.d.). The Crow Reservation has several defined rights with the oldest priority date listed for the tribe as July 25, 1868 (Crow Compact 2011). Among its many water-rights provisions, the agreement allows the Crow to take 500,000 acre-feet of flow from the Big Horn River, annually (Compact Implementation Program n.d.). Highlights in the Northern Cheyenne agreement include an October 1, 1881 priority date and, with some limits, the rights to 32,500 annual acre-feet of direct flow from the Tongue River.

Another set of water rights issues are also worthy of attention. Namely, issues regarding water availability and the rights of nonhuman entities. By the 1960s, irrigators, exercising their water rights, were known to completely de-water certain streams in the watershed during the late summer, and it was concerning to some people that the fish in public streams had no legal claim to water. *Murphy Rights* were approved by the legislature to protect Montana's Blue-Ribbon trout streams (Montana Department of Natural Resources and Conservation 2015a). With a December 1970 priority date, these water rights provided instream flow protections for 12 of Montana's rivers, including the Yellowstone River.

Further protections for instream flows were established for the Yellowstone River and its tributary streams in the late 1970s, 1980s, and 1990s (Water Policy Interim Committee 2018). However, there is no clear scientific basis for establishing flow thresholds (Bradford and Heinonen 2008), and the State of Montana has not set specific parameters for how to determine the minimum flow needed by fish. The limits of the instream flow protections have also not been fully vetted. For instance, irrigators were not asked to forgo withdrawals of water in 2016, even though the PKD outbreak discussed in Chapter 2 was, at least in part, a function of extremely low flows.

It is apparent that the resilience of the communities of the valley will depend on how water resources are shared. If we pause to think carefully about water rights, we might begin to wonder if we can afford to continue to think of all uses of water as equally beneficial. We might consider if, or how, we will accommodate claims as new or expanding water uses come into view. One resident from Billings complained at an open meeting, "Montana should stop handing out water appropriations" (Public Scoping Participant from Billings 2013). As it is, legislative and compact closures are enforced in some of the subbasins, which stops further allotments (Montana Department of Natural Resources and Conservation 2016), but in many circumstances, a water right can still be approved in the Yellowstone River Valley.

Our resilience will also be defined by how we manage drought. Within the agricultural communities of the valley, conservation ideals, commitments, and agendas are often drought sensitive (Horton et al. 2017), but only some irrigators have plans in place to address shortages:

> I think we're fairly prepared. We have water rationing plans in place, and the producers are well aware of them ... Everybody will be given less, a smaller allotment ... So, it's up to [each producer] to make a decision about what is economically best in terms of which crop you would like to save and which crop is going to suffer. So, it's the individual farmer that makes that decision in the end. I suppose [the rationing plan] has been in place for twenty years, but it's been fine-tuned a little bit more in the last seven or eight. (Farmer near Savage 2018)

Water rights are especially precious under conditions of overallocation, and any new water-dependent industry will need to find rights holders who are willing to forego, temporarily or permanently, their own interests in water allocations. It is notable that the producer's drought-mitigation plan, mentioned previously, applies only to a certain group of irrigators. The Yellowstone River Basin Water Plan (Montana Department of Natural Resources and Conservation 2014) calls for efforts to prepare for drought, more generally. However, little has been done to move this agenda forward. The state posts data concerning drought conditions each summer, but the most recent statewide drought plan was written over 25 years ago (Montana Department of Natural Resources and Conservation 1995).

Of interest is a key provision in the compact with the Crow Nation. Their agreement specifies commitments to "share shortages" during low water years (Compact Implementation Program n.d.). The shortages clause helped move the approval processes forward because it tempered the potential impact of the tribe's seniority rights on other rights holders during a time of drought. The clause also illuminates an important lesson: if one understands water as a shared resource, then one should also understand water shortage as a shared burden.

Many activities in the valley eventually return used water to the overall supply. In the language of water management, these are known as nonconsumptive uses. For example, the municipalities along the Yellowstone River that pull water directly from the river for their communities also return water to the river via their wastewater treatment plants. The returned portion is the nonconsumptive-use portion. The extensive irrigation projects of the valley are estimated to return 80 percent of their withdrawals via subsurface flows and return outlets (Cannon and Johnson 2004). In this way, water can be used again and again.

Now, let us return to the oil and gas fields. You will remember that drilling and hydraulic fracturing require water, and that in the Bakken region drilling companies need one to five million gallons of water per well. Since the 1950s, local farmers have sold water to the oil and gas companies. The drilling companies, most of which are headquartered in other states, do not wish to purchase water rights in Montana. Rather, they seek to simply purchase water in locations near their drilling sites.

Water sales are advantageous to the local farmers, who supplement their farm income by selling water, but not their water rights, to drilling companies. Farmers do not wish to sell their water-use rights because that would amount to a permanent transfer of the water right, and they would be left without a long-term future. They know that every oil boom eventually goes bust. When that happens, farmers simply go back to farming.

Yet, the sales between farmers and the oil and gas industry are often in violation of the water rights laws. Namely, water appropriated for irrigation purposes should not be used for oil and gas production. In some cases, the sales are from irrigation supplies and in some cases from groundwater wells generally permitted for livestock and/or household uses. During the Bakken boom (2000–2010), the practice of selling water for oil and gas development was so widespread that authorities could see no means to enforce the law. Instead, water authorities petitioned the legislature to change the law. It is now possible to request Temporary Permits that allow farmers to legally, temporarily, change the designated uses of their water rights. The code explicitly states, "Temporary uses include water needed for oil and gas exploration" (Water Policy Interim Committee 2018, 28).

There is, however, another important issue with these temporary water-right uses. Flood irrigation practices, as seen earlier in this case study, charge shallow aquifers and return a great deal of water back to the river itself (Figure 5.1). In contrast, drilling and hydraulic fracturing generally result in the permanent loss of water. Water that backflows from an oil or gas well is considered wastewater, and the drilling companies can permanently dispose of the wastewater as an industrial by-product. They do so because they consider it cost prohibitive to treat the water such that it could be used again. The wastewater is disposed of in deep wells, and it will never return to the overall water system. As such, drilling and hydraulic fracturing are generally considered consumptive water uses. Let us compare this consumptive use with agriculture's consumptive uses.

In 2014, total industrial uses of water in the Yellowstone River Basin, which include uses by the oil and gas industry, were estimated at over 32,000 acre-feet per year. However, as a percentage of the total withdrawals from the river, the industrial amount was calculated as less than

Figure 5.1 Flood irrigation, siphon tubes deliver water from irrigation ditch to rows of sugar beets

2 percent of all outtakes (Montana Department of Natural Resources and Conservation 2014, 104). In comparison, irrigation outtakes approached two million acre-feet. Assuming an 80 percent return rate, consumptive irrigation uses can be calculated as totaling approximately 366,000 acre-feet. Even if we assume the industrial uses are all consumptive (which they are not), those uses would total less than 10 percent of the consumptive use attributed to irrigation. It is little wonder, then, that during the water planning meetings, representatives from the oil and gas industry were unwilling to allow their industry to be singled out as a the "worst" consumptive users of water.

When considering the many beneficial uses that are potentially at risk during a water shortage, the valley's resilience will depend on the agricultural community's willingness to forgo, at least temporarily, some of their rightful outtakes. "Shared giving" is beginning to find its way into irrigators' conversations, but state laws make it difficult to offer water as a temporary gift (Anderson et al. 2016).

Our final perspective concerning water as a shared resource comes from the United Nations. As a vanguard of human rights, the United

Nations asks us to consider access to safe water to be a basic human right (Van de Lande 2015). We are asked to avoid the commodification of water or of the right to use water. The United Nations opposes cutting off water supplies, even when water bills are not paid. If we think beyond the overallocations of the Yellowstone River Valley and allow ourselves to ponder how we will ensure safe drinking water for 10 billion residents of Earth, the need to share water becomes much more than a local concern—it is a global human concern.

Channel Migration, Riparian Areas, and Flood Zones

Chapter 2 allowed us to narrow our focus to the plights of the Pallid Sturgeon and the cottonwood forests, but the overall health of the river system is much more unwieldy. Here, too, the desires and projects of humans play important roles, especially as human projects seemingly never cease. In the Yellowstone mainstem corridor, development near the river is continuously increasing (CEA 2015). People are charmed by the notion of a free-flowing river, one they imagine as unencumbered, and they want to live near it. As one realtor put it, "Riverfront property is worth a lot, but riverfront with a mountain view is worth the most" (Realtor in Paradise Valley 2008).

Given that undeveloped property is typically taxed at the lowest rate, community leaders are incentivized to allow development. Even a modest house on the river near Hysham will increase local coffers, let alone the multimillion-dollar homes that now populate the riverbanks in Paradise Valley. Thus, local leaders tend to see the economic well-being of their communities as tied to continued development (Robbins, Martin, and Gilbertz 2012). Areas near the river are more popular each year, but developers seldom consider the potential degradations to the river environments these projects will cause over time. Specifically, they rarely factor that development near the river often, either immediately or soon, comes at the expense of channel migration processes and riparian health.

Channel migration is the natural process of river channels changing course. Erosion (a gradual "chipping away" of a riverbank), avulsion (a sudden and profound change in the river course), and deposition (the creation or elongation of sand and gravel bars) are necessary for channel migration to occur (Florsheim, Mount, and Chin 2008). The process is most obvious after high water events. As explained by Hohensinner, Hauer, and Muhar (2018), changes in channel geometry are caused by fluctuating flows and sedimentation. They also discuss channel widening, braiding, and abandonment.

Along the Yellowstone River Valley, the directions and magnitudes of historical channel migrations have been mapped (CEA 2015). The maps also identify areas where the channel is likely to migrate next. Channel Migration Zones have been identified for the entire river corridor. Some Reaches are not expected to involve much migration, whereas others may well soon be sites of wholesale changes (e.g., compare Reach PC19 with Reach PC18). In some cases, the maps have already been proven accurate as predictors of channel movement. Importantly, channel migration is an important process in creating healthy riparian areas.

Riparian areas are produced when the river sweeps across a valley floor, enriching sites with surface and subsurface water and material flows (Gregory et al. 1991). When one flies in an airplane on a clear day, riparian areas are easy to identify. In the Yellowstone River Valley, the verdant path of the riparian areas is especially apparent (see Reaches D11 and D12), and from an overhead vantage, one can make out the contours of the river—sometimes as a single channel and sometimes as multiple channels. In many reaches, the sweep of the river covers acres and acres where channels form, reform, braid, and rebraid themselves (Figure 5.2). A civic leader explained a multichanneled area of the river in these terms, "It's meander-land, and nobody can own that" (City Official from Big Timber 2006).

Unencumbered channel migration promotes healthy ecological processes. For instance, erosion and avulsion introduce materials into the river, and the subsequent concentration of resources (rich soils and water) creates lush environments and habitats. Fallen trees and released soils contribute nutrients that the aquatic communities require. Debris can play an important role in creating structural habitats for spawning fish. Channel changes (and flooding) introduce temporarily saturated sandbars, hospitable to seedlings. Also, the complexity of the plant communities in riparian areas create varying types and structures of

Figure 5.2 The Yellowstone River where it meanders

habitat. Shading from trees reduces water temperatures, providing suitable habitat for fish and other animals (Knouft et al. 2021). Indeed, living on the riverbank allows residents to enjoy the aquatic, avian, and terrestrial communities of the riparian areas (Gilbertz, Horton, and Hall 2006). Whether they call it the riparian area or not—and very few do—residents love living in the heart of it. One resident described living with bears as if they were neighbors:

> Last year we had two bears that came through the yard... They were unaware that they were supposed to come out at night only and that they were supposed to fear humans. So, they were walking through the yard every day. They were drinking out of the water fountain in the flower garden, so I kept it full. I didn't want to disappoint them or make them angry. (Wildlife Enthusiast with Home on the Riverbank near Grey Cliff 2018)

When a function of an ecosystem is directly linked to human welfare, we refer to such capacities as ecosystem services (Fisher, Turner, and Morling 2009). In addition to supporting wildlife, riparian areas also provide ecosystem services to local residents, such as ensuring water quality and water availability (Machtinger 2007). For instance, riparian vegetation helps remove nitrates from river water (Maître et al. 2003) and helps reduce contamination of subsurface flows (Vidon, Welsh, and Hassanzadeh 2019). And although storage capacities of soils vary, flooded riparian areas have water retention capacities, essentially storing water that is slowly released back to the river via subsurface gravels (Gunnell et al. 2019). It is assumed that the totality of ecosystem services provided by riparian areas is not yet fully inventoried.

However, relations with the river's meanderings are not always congenial. The decisions of individuals and communities are often in conflict with the natural processes of the river. For example, landowners often want to protect their properties from erosion by putting riprap on their riverbank (a protective revetment). Over the decades, a great variety of techniques and materials have been used by landowners to "protect" their properties, including blocking side channels and stabilizing river bends with old cement slabs (Figure 5.3). One can even still find "parking lots" on the banks of the Yellowstone River—riverbanks where anchored car bodies line a riverbend.

Federal and state laws limit what landowners can do to protect their riverfront properties, but in emergency situations laws often allow for quick responses. Some owners have resorted to physically blocking the sudden progression of the river toward their homes and buildings, and authorities later deemed it a reasonable thing to do given the perceived jeopardy. Although these efforts appear to be effective, they may not be

Figure 5.3 Broken cement slabs as riprap

long-lived, and because there is often little or no engineering involved, such actions can easily result in unintended problems for neighbors or even for those who themselves took the emergency actions. Sadly, then, as landowners try to stem channel migration on their properties, they sometimes accelerate the rates of channel migration (Randle 2006). Subsequently, more property becomes "at risk," and more bank stabilization is installed. Property owners who cannot afford to stabilize their banks wonder how long it might be until the river endangers their homes or buildings. They feel threatened by the river. For others, the wait is over—the river has already taken their property (Reach A14; Gilbertz, Emerson, and Hall 2020; Figure 5.4).

Figure 5.4 The river under the house

Landowners hoping to stabilize their riverbanks must now secure state and federal permits, and they must use only approved materials, such as large granite boulders. The placement of these boulders must also follow strict guidelines to avoid "pushing" the erosion problem to a neighbor's property. Landowners, thus, typically must hire an engineer to design their projects, and they sometimes invest hundreds of thousands of dollars to stabilize only a few hundred feet of riverbank (Gilbertz, Horton, and Hall 2006). As one landowner described his frustrations about erosion of his property, it is clear he feels abused by the river, the rules, and the economics of his situation:

> I never know where my property line is at ... It's a wild and uncontrolled river, and the river takes a little every year. In real high-water years, its more aggressive. It takes fertile soil real fast ... It has worked its way into my meadows... and I've lost productive ground ... If I had substantial resources there might have been things that could have been done ... [but] the scale is overwhelming ... To restructure an old jetty and put in the riprap, it was three- to five-times the cost of the land ... I didn't have enough money. What could have I done? What should have I done? I'm not whining, I'm resigned ... I've resigned myself to this in sadness ... Free-flowing at whose cost? The people who want the river to run, where it wants to run, don't pay for it. I should be getting an award from the free-flowing folks because I've contributed a half-million in the form of lost land. (Agricultural Landowner near Columbus 2006)

Even those not personally affected can see the landowners' problems. An owner of a raft rental business, described the dilemmas this way:

> The thing about the Yellowstone is, it's such a meandering, naturally flowing river. It seeks all these little braids, and channels, and so on. So, it seems to work well over time. I know that people that have riverfront property get [nervous] when they start to get high water or floods and the natural erosion process takes place. And, whether it's cultivated land or not, people start putting in riprap

> to protect against erosion. [It] will actually change the water, away from just coming in and cutting into the bank ... But, if you do that over on one side of the river, maybe it just shoots it over and starts to do the same thing over on the other side of the river ... I'm not sure, but my suspicion is that when you start to mess around with it too much, then it's going to eliminate or degrade some of that natural structure and natural habitat. (Rafting Outfitter near Gardiner 2006)

As illustrated by the Physical Features Inventory of the Yellowstone River, protective projects, alterations meant to prevent river channel migration, are numerous throughout the valley (Explore Yellowstone n.d.). For example, much of the riverbank around Billings, a city of over 100,000 people, has been armored, and side-channels have been blocked. In one 6-mile stretch of the river (Reach B2), approximately 21,700 feet, or 4.1 miles, of bank armor has been put in place, and over 6,500 feet of side channels have been blocked (Reach Narrative B2 2015, 8). Nearby (Reach B3), another nearly 14,000 feet of side channels are blocked (Reach Narrative B3 2015, 12). In these areas, riparian functions have been essentially eliminated. Even where there are few structures and where development seems far less extensive than in the more urban areas, numerous bank stabilization and side-channel projects are completed each year. These projects are generally intended to protect property from flooding and erosion.

Another impact to riparian areas is caused when landowners shift the land to agricultural purposes. Known as land-use conversions, these changes can all rather wholly eliminate the riparian functions. In the lower valley, areas that were once densely populated with cottonwood forests are now used as cultivated fields (Reach D8). The spatial extent of these types of conversions, and the resulting decline in nesting habitats, have been calculated as a lost riparian function (CEA 2015).

Other impacts to channel migration and riparian areas are the result of flood control projects. The towns of Forsyth (Reach C10), Miles City (Reaches C16 and C17), and Glendive (Reaches D5 and D6) are all protected by levees. Unfortunately, in some cases the levees are no longer certified by the COE. Residents in these towns should carry federal flood insurance, but many of them do not. They believe the levees, in place since their grandparents lived in these towns, will not fail (Gilbertz, Emerson, and Hall 2020). Although the longevity of the levees is arguable, all of the levees affect riparian function. They tend to constrict the river into one channel by cutting off side channels and they eliminate channel migration processes that might occur if flooding were allowed.

Despite extensive costs and complex engineering, efforts to protect properties are sometimes in vain. In 1996 and 1997, high waters washed away many of the protections for Livingston residents whose homes were built on an island in the river (Reach PC14). Several homes were lost entirely to flooding that year, and others were all but lost (Figure 5.5). In the aftermath, dozens of landowners proposed armoring their properties. Today, where the river flows on the Livingston side of the island, various stabilization methods keep the river in a prescribed channel, and the river is constrained on both riverbanks (Reach PC14). More recently, flooding in 2018 threatened many of the valley's communities. It was feared that in Huntley—a town of just over 400 residents just east of Billings (Reach B5)—400 structures would be affected. Had the waters crested as expected, nearly the entire town would have been flooded. The flood threats are very real, in some years more immediately than in others.

Examples from the Missouri River help illustrate other issues with spring floods. Cities downstream of its confluence with the Mississippi

Figure 5.5 House on island after the floods took owner's yard

River, such as St. Louis and Memphis, are often in harm's way when spring runoff combines with spring rainstorms. Every year, the COE is faced with deciding where to direct flood waters so that damages will be minimized. Typically, a levy will be opened upriver from an urban area to disperse the water across the broader (historical) floodplain and reduce the potential for loss of property and life in the city. Not only are downstream areas then protected from immediate inundation, the water loses velocity, and its destructive power is greatly diminished. Less densely occupied areas are more likely to be sacrificed than urban areas. Of course, those residents whose properties are intentionally flooded are extremely upset; however, it makes good economic and humanitarian sense to direct flood waters to areas with the least development and the fewest numbers of people. In the future, similar calculations may be necessary in the Yellowstone River Valley.

Predictably, humans living near the river hope to stall flooding, erosion, and avulsion on their properties (Figure 5.6). Levies and bank armoring can be argued as building the resilience of the (human) community. However, these protections test the limits of our river system's resilience. We are drawn to rivers for all that they provide, but subsequent actions designed to protect investments in riverfront property endanger, ironically, the river system itself. Remember, it is reasonable to assume that had we stayed mostly out of the floodplains, channel migration zones, and riparian areas, both the Pallid Sturgeon and the cottonwood forests, as well as countless other animal and plant species, would be much better off.

Figure 5.6 Retirement home by the Yellowstone River

It is, perhaps, time to put less effort into protecting property and to put more consideration into protecting channel migration, riparian areas, and floodplains. At the very least, human interventions should be evaluated in terms of the unintended side effects and legacies that may cause new problems that ripple through river ecosystems (Hohensinner, Hauer, and Muhar 2018).

Final Thoughts About Resilience and Sustainability

Taken individually, our practices and actions seem quite reasonable. Yet, we know that we are slowly polluting our waters, and we know that with each successive project on the riverbanks we compromise the health of the riparian areas. So, although it is true that no one project or practice in a riparian area will wholly harm the river or its riparian health, it is also true that, cumulatively, flood control and bank stabilization efforts can significantly impair riparian processes and functions (CEA 2015). In the beginning pages of this book, we noted that underlying the pursuit of sustainability is the implicit charge to examine our practices willingly and critically. A river's resilience—its ability to withstand assaults—is not unlimited, and the Yellowstone River is no exception. Knowing that each project chips away at the river system's ability to function, we also know riparian health is at risk and that our ecosystem services are slipping away. In some places on the river, it is difficult to even pretend there is much "health" left. To what degree should we limit building in the flood zones, riparian areas, or channel migration zones?

If we do not act carefully, our economies, environment, and communities become much less sustainable and less resilient to foreseeable and unforeseeable adversities. The examples presented in this chapter—of water rights and river functions—make us aware of the profound complications involved in attending to the valley's long-term economic, environmental, and social well-being. Water is vital to every aspect of life in the valley (Figure 5.7). Our industries compete for supplies, the health of our environment depends on how well we manage our water resources, and our notions of fairness are complicated by a host of water laws that define access to opportunities. Even in 2006, local river enthusiasts were voicing caution:

> There's a direct tie between how well we manage all these activities and the health of the river. And that really is the problem that we face with the Yellowstone. Because none of these activities are benign in terms of the health of the river. (River Access Activist from Billings 2006)

Figure 5.7 The Yellowstone River near Terry

It is tempting to ask about thresholds, demarcations that would alert us to "go no further or risk ruin." We might think that we could better manage for sustainability and resilience if only we knew exactly how much we will have and how much we dare to take from the environment or from one another. However, as seen in this chapter, it is impossible to anticipate the totality of factors that would precisely define these thresholds. Worse, a history of human behavior has shown that identifying hypothesized thresholds effectively permits us to approach those limits, not knowing whether or not we miscalculated and have already surpassed a system's limits. It would be wiser to evaluate the direction in which we are headed and to make a course correction, if our path appears to lead us toward the ruin of our resources. Are we smart enough to change course? Do we have the resolve?

Discussion Questions

Regarding water rights:

1. Should we prioritize beneficial uses in Montana?
2. Should agriculture expect to continue with "business as usual" while fishing guides are asked to suspend their income-generating activities?
3. Should industries be allowed to permanently dispose of our water resources?
4. Will intense and/or prolonged droughts force us to consider new water-use rules?
5. Will we assure every resident of the valley access to good quality drinking water?
6. Is it fair to change the rules regarding water allocations?

Regarding the functions of riparian areas, we should ask:

1. Is riparian health wholly at risk in the Yellowstone River Valley?
2. Are we compromising the ecosystem services provided to us by the river so much that even our immediate needs are in jeopardy?

Given all that we have examined, we see that sustainability's central question is helpful, but not especially directive in local settings. Are we ready to ask better questions regarding the sustainability of the Yellowstone River Valley:

1. Is the Yellowstone River Valley moving toward or away from a resilient economy?
2. Will future generations in the valley inherit a more or less resilient and healthy natural environment?
3. Are communities in the valley moving toward improving resilience in terms of social fairness?
4. Are the communities in the valley moving toward overall resilience in terms of the complexities of the valley?

5. How might business models help agriculture, tourism, and the oil and gas industries incorporate complex sustainability goals into their operations?
6. In what ways are the residents' comments, from the various chapters, useful to sustainability advocates hoping to improve the resilience of their communities?

Easy Access Resources

Estimated Water Use in Montana in 2000: https://pubs.usgs.gov/sir/2004/5223/pdf/sir2004_5223.pdf

"How Are Instream Flows Protected?" Fact Sheet: https://static1.squarespace.com/static/5498382ce4b015fce7f847a2/t/57c7244c9f7456b915e34ccf/1472668777218/WaterFactSheets_ALL.pdf

Interactive Map of the Yellowstone River: http://montana.maps.arcgis.com/apps/webappviewer/index.html?id=3fc5b219f4494ebab2477e93a5bbecca

Impacts of Stabilization on the Yellowstone River-Reach B3: http://ftp.geoinfo.msl.mt.gov/Documents/Projects/Yellowstone_River_Clearinghouse/Yellowstone_Reach_Narratives_2015.pdf

"Montana Water Rights Protection Act" U.S. Senate Bill. www.congress.gov/bill/116th-congress/senate-bill/3019/text

Nonpoint Source Pollution: Agriculture: www.epa.gov/nps/nonpoint-source-agriculture

Tribal Water Rights, Montana's Summary: https://mtdnrc.maps.arcgis.com/apps/MapJournal/index.html?appid=63c5e165d5e34681a3cc3b7a615ab442

Reserved Water Rights for Indian Reservations, U.S. Department of Justice Summary: www.justice.gov/enrd/federal-reserved-water-rights-and-state-law-claims

Riparian Systems: www.nrcs.usda.gov/Internet/FSE_DOCUMENTS/nrcs143_010137.pdf

Water as a Human Right, United Nations: www.unwater.org/publications/eliminating-discrimination-inequalities-access-water-sanitation/

CHAPTER 6

Progress of Sustainability and Sustainability as Progress

Introduction

Only 50 years ago, United States elected officials enacted sweeping laws to protect endangered species (1969), water (1972), and air quality (1975–1990), and established the U.S. EPA (1970). To support the emerging rules, technical training in environmental fields grew, accelerating the advancement of science. During this same era, new academic disciplines, such as earth systems science and ecology, rapidly developed (Worster 1994). Later, academic fields began to integrate studies of the environment with societal and economic concerns. As examples, political ecology gained traction in the 1980s (Robbins 2004), while ecological economics (Røpke 2004) and industrial ecology (Erkman 1997) took shape in the 1990s. Beyond these new sciences, an important and profound postindustrial environmental consciousness emerged. This growing consciousness is consistently demonstrated in public opinion polls that show approximately two-thirds of U.S. adults state that environmental quality should be a priority, and the numbers are even higher among younger Americans (Funk and Kennedy 2020).

Despite this new environmental consciousness, much work remains in developing ways of thinking and scientific agendas that simultaneously address the needs of today and tomorrow. It is imperative that we engage in research that allows us to better understand how our actions affect human bodies, social systems, and ecosystems. As a broad vision, sustainability and sustainability sciences have been characterized as a new version of this needed progress (Peterson 1997). This version of progress focuses on designing human systems, so humans and other life will flourish on Earth forever (Ehrenfeld 2008). It involves changing ways of thinking to consider the interrelations among environmental, social, and economic systems, then changing our behaviors to abandon patterns that lead to decline in the quality of those systems.

We end our introduction to sustainability with a few brief discussions that we hope will lead you to consider your role in moving sustainability forward. In this chapter, we discuss two ways of thinking about sustainability agendas, the role of sustainability science, the role of people operating as engaged citizens, and the need for flexibility and steadfastness as dual elements of moving forward.

Thin and Thick Sustainability

The broadest vision of progress within sustainability calls on us to improve the quality of human life and environmental quality, all while improving the quality of both for future generations. This expansive vision, which implies moral obligations that easily garner widespread support, is described as *thin sustainability* (Miller 2013). Thin sustainability is a big notion. It is large enough for people to imagine how their businesses, skills, or desired futures belong within a sustainability agenda. People can easily rally around thin sustainability. As a broad concept, it is effective for gathering diverse people for a shared purpose. However, thin sustainability is commonly criticized as being too broad to translate into substantive action. The conceptual expansiveness of thin sustainability leaves subscribers with no agreed-upon definition, no substantive and specific meaning that prescribes particular actions. Thin sustainability visions are good for motivating conversations and mustering people toward a general mindset, but in order to roll up our sleeves and begin to make changes, a more detailed and nuanced, or thick, vision of sustainability is needed.

Thick sustainability is specific. It focuses on specific problems and specific system interactions. It is located in a place and is a product of persons who are local residents, who make their homes and businesses in that environment (Miller 2013). Thick sustainability works toward building a concrete, site-specific vision for sustainability agendas that will make a difference in a particular environment for a distinct set of people. By focusing attention on a refined perspective of a system and its problems, a community can design explicit actions. Pursuing thick sustainability begins when the community accepts and examines the complex interactions among its social, environmental, and economic systems. Thick sustainability proceeds, then, to shape human behaviors to improve the functioning of specific systems.

This book introduces sustainability notions through the telling of system interactions within a specific watershed, and our discussions were informed by the voices of community members who live in this large river valley in the arid American West. The examples in this book demonstrate how broad notions, thin sustainability, allow diverse interests to generally agree upon some paths forward. However, the examples also illustrate that identifiable problems can only be addressed when visions of sustainability emerge in context, specific to a place, its ecological systems (riparian cottonwood forests and sturgeon fish habitat), climate–hydrology systems (precipitation patterns and flood and drought cycles), and the societies, rules, and economies available for living there (farming, recreation, oil and gas extraction, and water rights). Engaging in business and community development that is sustainable emerges when we develop thick visions of sustainability, such as examining specific human and environmental system interactions associated with floods, flood control, cottonwood forests, and societal demands for residential, municipal, and agricultural development.

On the Yellowstone River, the CEA, with its biophysical, economic, social, and cultural data analyses, accomplished the first stages of providing thickly detailed background information needed for decision making. Important work remains to be done as the people of the Yellowstone River Valley move from thin to thick sustainability perspectives and as they begin to address pressing sustainability challenges meaningful to particular river reaches and the entire valley. It is here, at this juncture in the story of the Yellowstone River Valley, where sustainability science can be of help.

Sustainability Science

Researchers working in international development in the 1990s recognized that to deal with complex intertwined problems, they needed scientific approaches that combined the natural and social sciences. In applied academic fields addressing sustainability, traditional disciplines were tending to become more interdisciplinary to address problems in the systems in which they worked (Kajikawa, Saito, and Takeuchi 2017). A new field of research and university education, sustainability science, emerged. This new area of study used a broad array of university research areas to develop novel approaches for addressing pressing sustainability challenges. Beyond advancing disciplinary knowledge, the aim of sustainability science is to *solve problems* (Kates et al. 2001). Sustainability science research examines the interactions between natural and social systems and how those interactions affect the challenges of sustainability: meeting the needs of present and future generations, while substantially reducing poverty and conserving the planet's life support systems (National Research Council 2011).

Two principles guide sustainability science. The first is that to address complex problems, interdisciplinary teams of social and natural scientists must work together to create detailed understandings of human–environmental systems. Second, the knowledge generated by these teams should lead to actions that move communities toward improving the projected long-term health of their local systems (Wiek et al. 2012). For such knowledge to be actionable, members of local communities must be consulted as experts of their home systems. Local communities must be actively involved in designing the improvements. As illustrated throughout the book, long-term residents know what has been tried in the past. They know what ideas will be rejected by their neighbors. They know who to talk to and who must be involved for any decision-making process to be successful. Problems cannot be successfully addressed by outsider experts unless they engage local communities.

Role of People as Engaged Citizens

Sustainability is not a static destination but, rather, a moving target. It requires a community to develop a vision for themselves and for future generations that acknowledges change as a fundamental and necessary dynamic in the local environment. Local people must embrace being adaptive, especially in the face of unforeseen challenges. Their vision determines which actions are needed now, and which actions can be postponed. Groups of residents and leaders must define what matters to them based on context, resources, and people (Norton and Thompson 2014). Sustainable behaviors are the behaviors that help the community get from the current state to their stated community-defined vision of thick sustainability (Figure 6.1).

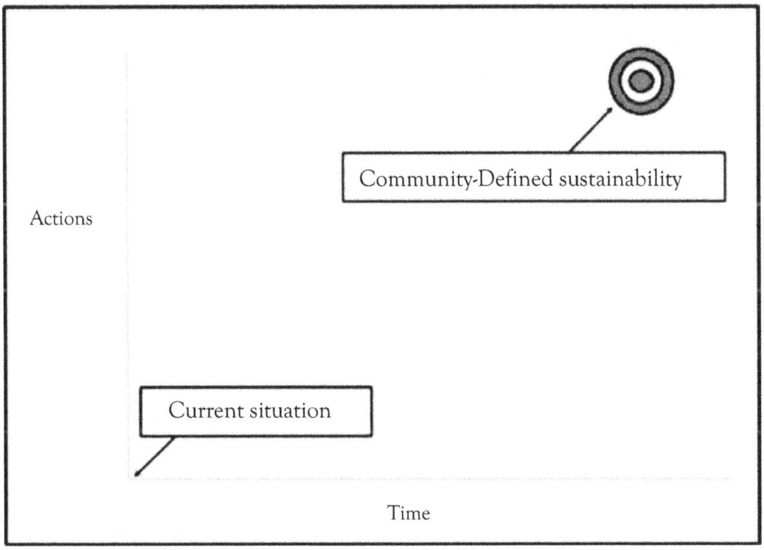

Figure 6.1 Thick sustainability is a community-defined goal. The actions needed are those that get a community from the current situation to its vision of sustainability

Thick sustainability is a community-defined goal. The actions needed are those that help move a community from its current situation toward its vision of sustainability.

Sustainability scientists, and other outside experts, can make worthwhile contributions to helping communities reach their sustainability goals; however, this kind of input from outsiders must be accompanied by an understanding of complex systems (including the specific systems in place within the community in question) and the ability to explain complexity in ways that help communities understand their functioning within these systems. Once clear about the specific needs faced by a community, the local community members can develop community-defined goals that are specific to place, local economies, local values, and local ambitions. Then, while still working with outside experts, the community can identify paths for achieving their sustainability goals. These efforts require coordination and good listening, especially among business and community leaders, researchers, and governmental officials. Outside experts can help local groups understand technical parts of the system for orienting to their goals, but the community must actively define their goals, navigate local terrains (physical, cultural, and political), and help make necessary course corrections. Any proposed rules, or changes to rules, must be meaningful to those expected to follow them.

The Yellowstone CEA is an example of an integrated research effort, made up of both outsider experts and insider community participants, designed to better understand a complex system. Although the research was conducted in a traditional piecemeal fashion (e.g., wildlife biologists inventoried birds and hydrologists assessed floodplain condition), the CEA constitutes a clearinghouse of the biological, hydrological, and geomorphological past and current conditions along the river. The data include the Yellowstone River Physical Features Inventory and the YRCI, both which help document the activities, goals, and desires of the people of the valley in terms of past and present individual, familial, and community perspectives.

Now that the reports are filed, we have a much better understanding, from a scientific perspective, of the river, its functions, systems, and people. Few communities have access to this level of environmental and social data. Moreover, the data, and researcher's interpretations of that data, are freely available to the public. The Montana DNRC and the YRCDC have ensured public accessibility of the data, both in terms of physical access and ease of understanding. Decisions concerning how to best use this knowledge to shape behaviors, to reflect locally held values and desired futures, is the work of communities. Whether they call this work sustainability or not does not matter. What matters is that the community is taking steps toward developing the community-defined visions of sustainability necessary for valley communities to enhance their resilience in the face of current and unforeseen changes—but there is still much work to be done.

What to Keep and What to Let Go?

In Chapter 5, we discussed how resilience is the capacity of a natural system or human community to be able to withstand a disturbance and remain viable with its key elements intact. With each disturbance, a resilient system does change, but it retains its core identity. Knowing what we know now from the CEA, the work of building resilience of resource-dependent livelihoods in an ever-changing (dynamic) system like the Yellowstone River Valley requires difficult conversations and tough decisions about what behaviors best fit the specific social and ecological realities of the valley and which behaviors no longer work (or never worked).

Daniel Lerch (2017) writes that building resilience involves "intentionally guiding a system's process of adaptation so as to preserve some qualities and allow others to fade away, all while retaining the essence—or identity—of the system" (5). Identity is determined by humans in terms of what they value and where they live. Local people are always the heart of planning for resilience. In the Yellowstone River Valley, because agriculture, recreation, real estate, and tourism depend on the river, local people must come together to colead conversations with civic leaders about what qualities of valley life should be preserved and which land-use practices should be allowed (encouraged) to fade away. Sustainability involves making hard choices about what behaviors need to be kept and which ones should be abandoned because they are no longer relevant to the changing systems we live within.

The CEA reveals how some land-use behaviors in the Yellowstone River Valley are outmoded when examined in light of what the residents themselves have stated they appreciate and wish to preserve. For example, bank stabilization projects (e.g., rip-rap) have a cumulative impact on fish habitats. Thus, projects that fail to meet the community's priorities, based on current understanding of the complex interactions in the system, should be replaced with ones that do. Rather than just addressing the immediate and single-priority impacts (e.g., preventing river meanders), projects should be designed to identify and account for systemwide impacts (e.g., riparian function, cottonwood forests, fish habitat, fishing and guiding livelihoods, and tourism industry). The CEA also reveals how other behaviors need to be reconfigured if the river is to remain a vital element of valley residents' lives. It is at the intersection of articulated community values and scientific evidence where working together, challenging conversations, and hard choices occur.

Changing behaviors is arduous. Encouraging voluntary compliance requires a lot of educating. Alternatively, policy—legal rule changes—may be an easier route for communities to take to ensure that any behaviors misaligned with the community's values fade away. Laws are mutual coercion, mutually agreed upon (Hardin 1968). Environmental laws manage human behaviors. They are administered through incentives (carrots) to comply with agreed-upon behavior changes or through punishment, such as fines, for noncompliance (sticks). Laws often cover large geographical spaces, like a U.S. state or a river valley, and are generally accompanied by the resources of government and technical expertise to administer the incentives or fines. Policies for shared resources, like those of the Yellowstone River, are where values and science must meet. We must be willing to adopt new behaviors and rules, and we must be willing to abandon notions that prohibit us from achieving our goals.

Our task is to figure this out: what do we keep, and what do we let go? If yesterday's thinking led to today's problems, then repeating yesterday's thinking may not help us find the solutions we need. Our taken-for-granted behaviors and logics should be examined and, perhaps, wholly abandoned if we intend to protect resources such as water, air, and biodiversity for future generations. Sustainability's success depends on understanding the complexity of our systems, the interrelatedness of our problems, and the core identities of our communities. This is the ambition of sustainability and the science of sustainability. There is tremendous opportunity for individuals, businesses, and society to contribute to building more sustainable communities and natural systems. Please, go, help shape our future.

Discussion Questions

1. How can we use sustainability science to inform a local public?
2. Who must be engaged for a local community to move toward a coherent and *thick* vision of sustainability?
3. How might current views concerning ecosystems forestall a *thick* sustainability agenda?

4. How might current views concerning local economies forestall a *thick* sustainability agenda?
5. How might current views concerning fairness forestall a *thick* sustainability agenda?
6. In complex systems, how do we begin to organize policy decisions?
7. How would you define the needed philosophies that businesses, communities, and governmental entities must adopt if they hope to encourage *thick* sustainability?
8. How do you define your role in helping your community develop a *thick* sustainability agenda?

Disclaimer

The development of this case study was supported in part by the National Science Foundation (NSF; project numbers 1726834, 1726278, 1726843), the U.S. Army Corps of Engineers (USACE; W9128F18P0084, W9182F18Q0037), and the USDA National Institute of Food and Agriculture, McIntire Stennis, project 1021674. The content is solely the responsibility of the authors and does not necessarily represent the official views of the NSF, USCOE, or USDA.

References

Adamson, J., M.M. Evans, R. Stein, and K. Piselle, eds. 2002. *The Environmental Justice Reader: Politics, Poetics, and Pedagogy*. Tucson, AZ: The University of Arizona Press.

Amlin, N.A., and S.B. Rood. 2001. "Inundation Tolerances of Riparian Willows and Cottonwoods." *Journal of the American Water Resources Association* 37, no. 6, pp. 1709–1720. https://doi.org/10.1111/j.1752-1688.2001.tb03671.x

Anderson, M.B., L. Ward, S.J. Gilbertz, J. McEvoy, and D.M. Hall. 2018. "Prior Appropriation and Water Planning Reform in Montana's Yellowstone River Basin: Path Dependency or Boundary Object?" *Journal of Environmental Policy & Planning* 20, no. 2, pp. 198–213. https://doi.org/10.1080/1523908X.2017.1348286

Anderson, M.B., L. Ward, J. McEvoy, S.J. Gilbertz, and D.M. Hall. 2016. "Developing the Water Commons? The (Post) political Condition and the Politics of 'Shared Giving' in Montana." *Geoforum* 74, pp. 147–157. https://doi.org/10.1016/j.geoforum.2016.06.002

Auble, G.T., and M.L. Scott. 1998. "Fluvial Disturbance Patches and Cottonwood Recruitment Along the Upper Missouri River, Montana." *Wetlands* 18, pp. 546–556. https://doi.org/10.1007/BF03161671

Auble, G., M.L. Scott, J. Frazier, C. Krause, and M.F. Merigliano. 2005. "Cottonwood in the Missouri Breaks National Monument." *Fact Sheet 2005–3132*, Reston, VA: U.S. Geological Survey. https://doi.org/10.3133/fs20053132

Bach, R. 1982. "The Yellowstone River Compact: An Overview." *Public Land and Resources Law Review* 3, 179–193. https://scholarship.law.umt.edu/plrlr/vol3/iss1/8/

Backes, M. February 17, 2020. *Senior Biologist, Montana Pallid Sturgeon Recovery Team. Lecture for Montana State University Billings' Environmental Studies students, February Field Day*. Miles City, MT: Montana Fish, Wildlife and Parks, Miles City Regional Office.

Bakken, G.M. 2011. *The Mining Law of 1872: Past, Present and Prospects*. Albuquerque, NM: University of New Mexico Press. https://muse.jhu.edu/book/17768

Bakken, S. n.d. "Bakken Shale Companies and Active Operators." B*akken Shale: News, Marketplace, Jobs*. https://bakkenshale.com/companies/ (accessed June 26, 2020).

Beattie, A. June 16, 2019. "The 3 Pillars of Corporate Sustainability." *Investopedia*, www.investopedia.com/articles/investing/100515/three-pillars-corporate-sustainability.asp

Berry, T. 2000. *The Great Work: Our Way into the Future.* New York, NY: Bell Tower.

Bertocchi, G. 2006. "The Law of Primogeniture and the Transition from Landed Aristocracy to Industrial Democracy." *Journal of Economic Growth* 11, pp. 43–70. https://doi.org/10.1007/s10887-006-7405-4

Board of Governors. 2019. *Report on the Economic Well-Being of U.S. Households in 2018.* Washington DC: Board of Governors of the Federal Reserve System.

Borman, M., and L. Larson. 2002. "Cottonwood Establishment, Survival, and Stand Characteristics." EM880. Corvallis, OR: University of Oregon Extension Service. https://catalog.extension.oregonstate.edu/sites/catalog/files/project/pdf/em8800.pdf

Braatne, J.H., R. Jamieson, K.M. McGill, and S.B. Rood. 2007. "Instream Flows and the Decline of Riparian Cottonwoods Along the Yakima River, Washington, USA." *River Research and Applications* 23, no. 3, pp. 247–267. https://doi.org/10.1002/rra.978

Bradford, M.J., and J.S. Heinonen. 2008. "Low Flows, Instream Flow Needs and Fish Ecology in Small Streams." *Canadian Water Resources Journal* 33, no. 2, pp. 165–180. https://doi.org/10.4296/cwrj3302165

Brown, M. February 02, 2015. "Lawsuit Filed Over Fate of Dinosaur-like River Fish." *Billings Gazette, Associated Press.* https://billingsgazette.com/news/local/lawsuit-filed-over-fate-of-dinosaur-like-river-fish/article_fded1176-7a0f-5cad-bc44-cd981def5382.html

Brundtland Commission. 1987. *Our Common Future: The World Commission on Environment and Development.* Oxford, UK: Oxford University Press.

Cannon, M.R., and D.R. Johnson. 2004. "Estimated Water Use in Montana in 2000." *Scientific Investigations Report 2004–5223.* Denver, CO: U.S. Geological Survey in cooperation with the Montana Department of Natural Resources and Conservation. https://pubs.usgs.gov/sir/2004/5223/pdf/sir2004_5223.pdf

Chaney, R. 2016. "New Trouble in Paradise: Yellowstone Fish-kill Revives Fears of Whirling Disease." *Independent Record*, https://helenair.com/news/state-and-regional/new-trouble-in-paradise-yellowstone-fish-kill-revives-fears-of/article_806e8e18-1ffe-558c-b503-3059a3bfab38.html

Chase, K.J. 2014. "Streamflow Statistics for Unregulated and Regulated Conditions for Selected Locations on the Upper Yellowstone and Bighorn Rivers, Montana and Wyoming, 1928–2002." *Scientific Investigations Report 2014–5115.* Reston, VA: U.S. Geological Survey. http://dx.doi.org/10.3133/sir20145115

Compact Implementation Program. n.d. "Montana Water Right Compacts (A Bird's Eye View)." Helena, MT: Montana Department of Natural Resources and Conservation. https://mtdnrc.maps.arcgis.com/apps/MapJournal/index.html?appid=63c5e165d5e34681a3cc3b7a615ab442 (accessed June 30, 2020).

Constitution of the State of Montana, Article IX, Section 3. 1972. https://courts.mt.gov/portals/189/library/docs/72constit.pdf

Cooper, D.T., and D.F. Van Haverbeke. 1990. "Populus Deltoides." In *Silvics of North America*, Technical Coordinated by R.M. Burns, and B.H. Honkala. Agriculture Handbook 654, Vol. 2. Washington DC: U.S. Department of Agriculture, Forest Service. www.srs.fs.usda.gov/pubs/misc/ag_654/volume_2/populus/deltoides.htm

Cornes, R., and T. Sandler. 1986. *The Theory of Externalities, Public Goods, and Club Goods*. Cambridge UK: Cambridge University Press.

Cramer, R. February 28, 2020. "Park County Court Cases Testing Boundaries of Public Access, Private Property Rights." *Yellowstone Public Radio, Environment & Science*, Broadcast. www.ypradio.org/environment-science/2020-02-28/park-county-court-cases-testing-boundaries-of-public-access-private-property-rights

Crow Compact, Appendix 3: Listing by Owner. March 04, 2011. Montana Department of Natural Resources and Conservation, Water Compact Implementation Program, http://dnrc.mt.gov/divisions/water/water-compact-implementation-program/docs/compact-appendices/crow_appendix_3.pdf

Daily, G.C., and P.R. Ehrlich. 1992. "Population, Sustainability, and Earth's Carrying Capacity." In *Ecosystem Management*, eds. F.B. Samson and F.L. Knopf, 435–450. New York, NY: Springer. https://doi.org/10.1007/978-1-4612-4018-1_32

Dalby, C. September 05, 2018. "Upper Yellowstone River Surface-Water Supply and Trends." Montana Department of Natural Resources and Conservation, Upper Yellowstone River Workshop Slides, www.researchgate.net/profile/Chuck_Dalby/publication/339238344_Upper_Yellowstone_River_Surface-Water_Supply_and_Trends/links/5e7b727c299bf1a91b77d5e6/Upper-Yellowstone-River-Surface-Water-Supply-and-Trends.pdf

Danylchuk, A.J., J. Tiedemann, and S.J. Cooke. 2017. "Perceptions of Recreational Fisheries Conservation Within the Fishing Industry: Knowledge Gaps and Learning Opportunities Identified at East Coast Trade Shows in the United States." *Fisheries Research* 186 (Part 3), pp. 681–687. https://doi.org/10.1016/j.fishres.2016.05.015

Defenders of Wildlife. n.d. "Our Approach." *Our Work*. https://defenders.org/our-work (accessed June 26, 2020).

Deutsch, M. 1975. "Equity, Equality, and Need: What Determines Which Value Will Be Used as the Basis of Distributive Justice?" *Journal of Social Issues* 31, no. 3, pp. 137–149. https://doi.org/10.1111/j.1540-4560.1975.tb01000.x

Dick, T.A. 1996. "Huntley Project." U.S. Bureau of Reclamation Report. www.usbr.gov/projects/pdf.php?id=126

DiLallo, M. July 11, 2018. "The Five Companies Dominating the Bakken Shale Play." *The Motley Fool.* www.fool.com/investing/2016/08/13/the-5-companies-dominating-the-bakken-shale-play.aspx

Dixon, M.D., W.C. Johnson, M.L. Scott, D. Bowen, and L.A. Rabbe. 2012. "Dynamics of Plains Cottonwood (*Populus deltoides*) Forests and Historical Landscape Change Along Unchannelized Segments of the Missouri River, USA." *Environmental Management* 49, no. 5, pp. 990–1008. https://doi.org/10.1007/s00267-012-9842-5

Dyllick, T., and K. Hockerts. 2002. "Beyond the Business Case for Corporate Sustainability." *Business Strategy and the Environment* 11, no. 2, 130–141. https://onlinelibrary.wiley.com/doi/abs/10.1002/bse.323

Dyllick, T., and K. Muff. 2016. "Clarifying the Meaning of Sustainable Business: Introducing a Typology from Business-as-Usual to True Business Sustainability." *Organization & Environment* 29, no. 2, pp. 156–174. https://doi.org/10.1177/1086026615575176

Ehrenfeld, J. 2008. *Sustainability by Design: A Subversive Strategy for Transforming our Consumer Culture.* London, UK: Yale University Press.

Eizenberg, E., and Y. Jabareen. 2017. "Social Sustainability: A New Conceptual Framework." *Sustainability* 9, no. 1, p. 68. https://doi.org/10.3390/su9010068

Elkington, J. 1997. *Cannibals with Forks: The Triple Bottom Line of 21st-Century Business.* New York, NY: John Wiley & Son Ltd.

Emerson, M.R., D.M. Hall, and S.J. Gilbertz. 2021. "Pipeline Pipedreams: Oil Spills, Pipeline Accidents, and the Local Truths Embedding Fossil Fuels in the Yellowstone River Valley, United States." *Energy Research & Social Science* 72, p. 101859. https://doi.org/10.1016/j.erss.2020.101859

Energy and Environmental Research Center. n.d. "Water Consumption in the Bakken." Beyond the Boom. Next-Generation Science and Engineering Opportunities to Optimize the Bakken Petroleum System. Bakken Production Optimization Program. University of North Dakota, Energy and Environmental Research Center. https://undeerc.org/Bakken/Water-Consumption-in-the-Bakken.aspx (accessed June 26, 2020).

Erkman, S. 1997. "Industrial Ecology: An Historical View." *Journal of Cleaner Production* 5, nos. pp. 1–2, 1–10. https://doi.org/10.1016/S0959-6526(97)00003-6

"Explore Yellowstone River Physical Features." n.d. Story maps, produced in conjunction with the Cumulative Effects Analysis, housed at the Montana State Library's Yellowstone River Corridor Clearinghouse. https://montana.maps.arcgis.com/apps/MapSeries/index.html?appid=3bfe4845f1964d5b827f2e4fe5c7f914 (accessed February 12, 2021).

Fisher, B., R.K. Turner, and P. Morling. 2009. "Defining and Classifying Ecosystem Services for Decision Making." *Ecological Economics* 68, no. 3, pp. 643–653. https://doi.org/10.1016/j.ecolecon.2008.09.014

Fleishman, E., J.R. Thomson, R.M. Nally, D.D. Murphy, and J.P. Day. 2005. "Using Indicator Species to Predict Species Richness of Multiple Taxonomic Groups." *Conservation Biology* 9, no. 4, pp. 1125–1137. https://doi.org/10.1111/j.1523-1739.2005.00168.x

Fleming, J., and R.J. Ledogar. 2008. "Resilience, An Evolving Concept: A Review of Literature Relevant to Aboriginal Research." *Pimatisiwin* 6, no. 2, 7–23. www.ncbi.nlm.nih.gov/pmc/articles/PMC2956753/

Florsheim, J.L., J.F. Mount, and A. Chin. 2008. "Bank Erosion as a Desirable Attribute of Rivers." *BioScience* 58, no. 6, pp. 519–29. https://doi.org/10.1641/B580608

Food and Agriculture Organization of the United Nations. June 19, 2020. "The State of World Fisheries and Aquaculture, 2020. In Brief." *Sustainability in Action*. Rome, Italy: Food and Agriculture Organization of the United Nations. https://doi.org/10.4060/ca9231en

French, B. December 27, 2020. "Summer Survey Provides Insight to Paradise Valley River Use." *Billings Gazette*, Section D., Montana Untamed: Insights into Paradise, D-1-2. https://billingsgazette.com/outdoors/summer-survey-provides-insight-to-paradise-valley-river-use/article_1a5a90f0-02a5-568e-a31d-e9b75fb1c932.html

Friedman, J.M., and E.R. Griffin. February 2017. "Management of Plains Cottonwood at Theodore Roosevelt National Park, North Dakota." *Natural Resource Report NPS/THRO/NRR—2017/1395*. Fort Collins, CO: U.S. Department of the Interior, National Park Service, Natural Resource Stewardship and Science. https://irma.nps.gov/DataStore/DownloadFile/566427

Funk, C., and B. Kennedy. 2020. "How Americans See Climate Change and the Environment in 7 Charts." *Pew Research Center*. Fact Tank: News in the Numbers. www.pewresearch.org/fact-tank/2020/04/21/how-americans-see-climate-change-and-the-environment-in-7-charts/

Gilbertz, S.J., M.B. Anderson, and J.M. Adkins. 2021. "The Bakken Blind Field: An Empirical Investigation of Planetary Urbanization and Opaqueness in the Oil and Gas Fields of Eastern Montana, USA." *Annals of the American Association of Geographers* 111, no. 2, pp. 591–608. https://doi.org/10.1080/24694452.2020.1774351

Gilbertz, S.J., E.K. Austin, J. Norton, C. Horton, and D. Hall. 2011. "Wicked Wisdoms: Illuminations of Conceptual Capacities among Local Leaders of the Yellowstone River." *Studies in Sociology of Science* 2, no. 2, 1–10. http://dx.doi.org/10.3968/j.sss.1923018420110202.041

Gilbertz, S.J., M. Emerson, and D. Hall. April 2020. "Yellowstone River Cultural Inventory—2012: Summary Report of all Segments." Co-Sponsored by the Yellowstone River Conservation District Council with Funding from the U.S. Army Corps of Engineers. http://ftp.geoinfo.msl.mt.gov/Documents/Projects/Yellowstone_River_Clearinghouse/YRCI_2012_SUMMARY_REPORT_of_ALL_SEGMENTS_FINAL_wPubDate.pdf

Gilbertz, S.J., D.M. Hall, and L.C. Ward. September, 2013. *Yellowstone Basin Advisory Council: Membership & Report of 2013 Public Scoping Activities.* Helena, MT: Montana Department of Natural Resources and Conservation. http://dnrc.mt.gov/divisions/water/management/docs/state-water-plan/yellowstone/scoping-report/scoping_report.pdf

Gilbertz, S.J., D.M. Hall, L.C. Ward, and M.B. Anderson. 2019. "Science on the Sideline: Pragmatism and the Yellowstone River Basin Advisory Council." *Water Resources Management* 33, no. 4, pp. 1411–1424. https://doi.org/10.1007/s11269-019-02207-w

Gilbertz, S.J., C. Horton, and D.M. Hall. 2006. "Yellowstone River Cultural Inventory—2006: Overall Summary Report with River-Length Interest Group Analyses." Sponsored by the Yellowstone River Conservation District Council with funding from the U.S. Army Corps of Engineers. http://ftp.geoinfo.msl.mt.gov/Documents/Projects/Yellowstone_River_Clearinghouse/YRCI_2006_OVERALL_SUMMARY.pdf

Gloege, M. 2007. *Survival or Gradual Extinction: The Small Town in the Great Plains of Eastern Montana.* Corvallis, OR: Meadowlark Publishing Services.

Grau, K. October 01, 2018. "2017 Economic Contribution of Nonresident Travel Spending in Montana Regions and Counties." Research Report 2018-13. Bozeman, MT: Institute for Tourism and Recreation Research Publications, University of Montana: Bozeman. https://scholarworks.umt.edu/cgi/viewcontent.cgi?article=1374&context=itrr_pubs

Gregory, S.V., F.J. Swanson, W.A. McKee, and K.W. Cummins. 1991. "An Ecosystem Perspective of Riparian Zones: Focus on Links between Land and Water." *BioScience* 41, no. 8, pp. 540–551. https://doi.org/10.2307/1311607

Gro Intelligence. June 11, 2018. "A Look at Fertilizer and Pesticide Use in the US." *Insights.* https://gro-intelligence.com/insights/a-look-at-fertilizer-and-pesticide-use-in-the-us#Fertilizer

Gunderson, L.H. 2000. "Ecological Resilience—In Theory and Application." *Annual Review of Ecology and Systematics* 31, 425–39. www.jstor.org/stable/221739

Gunnell, K., M. Mulligan, R.A. Francis, and D.G. Hole. 2019. "Evaluating Natural Infrastructure for Flood Management Within the Watersheds of

Selected Global Cities." *Science of The Total Environment* 670, pp. 411–424. https://doi.org/10.1016/j.scitotenv.2019.03.212

Haggerty, J., P.H. Gude, M. Delorey, and R. Rasker. 2014. "Long Term Effects of Income Specialization in Oil and Gas Extraction: The U.S. West, 1980–2011." *Energy Economics* 45, pp. 186–95. https://doi.org/10.1016/j.eneco.2014.06.020.

Hall, D.M., S.J. Gilbertz, M.B. Anderson, P.M. Avellaneda, D.L. Ficklin, J.H. Knouft, and C.S. Lowry. 2021. "Mechanisms for Engaging Social Systems in Freshwater Science Research." *Freshwater Science* 40, no. 1, pp. 245–251. https://doi.org/10.1086/713039

Hall, D.M., S.J. Gilbertz, M.B. Anderson, and L.C. Ward. 2016. "Beyond 'Buy-in': Designing Citizen Participation in Water Planning as Research." *Journal of Cleaner Production* 133, pp. 725–734. https://doi.org/10.1016/j.jclepro.2016.05.170

Hall, D.M., S.J. Gilbertz, C.C. Horton, and T.R. Peterson. 2012. "Culture as a Means to Contextualize Policy." *Journal of Environmental Studies and Sciences* 2, no. 3, pp. 222–233. https://doi.org/10.1007/s13412-012-0077-9

Hall, D.M., T.M. Swannack, E.D. Lazarus, M.J. Peterson, S.J. Gilbertz, C.C. Horton, and T.R. Peterson. 2015. "Integrating Social Power and Political Influence into Models of Social-Ecological Systems." *European Journal of Sustainable Development* 4, no. 2, pp. 61–76. https://doi.org/10.14207/ejsd.2015.v4n2p61

Hardin, G. 1968. "The Tragedy of the Commons." *Science* 162, no. 3859, pp. 1243–1248.

Healy, S. June 19–23, 2006. "Cultural Resilience, Identity and the Restructuring of Political Power in Bolivia." Paper Submitted for the 11th Biennial Conference of the International Association for the Study of Common Property, Bali, Indonesia. https://dlc.dlib.indiana.edu/dlc/bitstream/handle/10535/1488/Healey_susan.pdf?sequence=1

Heman, H.H. 1949. "Water Rights under the Law of Montana." *Montana Law Review* 10, no. 1, 13–22. https://scholarship.law.umt.edu/mlr/vol10/iss1/2

Hennip, R.D. 1973. "History of the Crude Oil Industry in Montana." *Graduate Student Theses, Dissertations, & Professional Papers*. 5846. Master of Business Administration thesis, University of Montana: Missoula. https://scholarworks.umt.edu/etd/5846

Herbaugh, H. July 14, 2019. "Intake Project Construction Begins." *Glendive Ranger Review*, www.rangerreview.com/content/intake-project-construction-begins.

Hohensinner, S., C. Hauer, and S. Muhar. 2018. "River Morphology, Channelization, and Habitat Restoration." In *Riverine Ecosystem Management: Science towards Governing for a Sustainable Future*, eds S. Schmutz and J. Sendzimir, 41–65. Aquatic Ecology Series, vol. 8. Cham, Switzerland: Springer. https://doi.org/10.1007/978-3-319-73250-3_3

Holloway, W.L., and Supreme Court Justice, October 24, 1921. "Opinion." Montana Supreme Court, *Mettler v. Ames Realty Co.*, 61 Mont. 152, 201, 157–171. https://cite.case.law/mont/61/152/?highlight=Codified+Statutes+of+1872+as+Chapter+34%2C+with+the+addition+of+section+11

Horton, C.C., S.J. Gilbertz, D.M. Hall, and T.R. Peterson. 2019. "Negotiating the Democratic Paradox: Approaches Drawn from Governance Efforts on Yellowstone River." *Frontiers in Communication* 4, p. 25. https://doi.org/10.3389/fcomm.2019.00025

Horton, C., D. Hall, S. Gilbertz, and T. Peterson. 2017. "Voice as Entry to Agriculturalists' Conservationist Identity: A Cultural Inventory of the Yellowstone River." *Environmental Communication* 11, no. 5, pp. 609–623. https://doi.org/10.1080/17524032.2016.1157505

Jean, R. April 05, 2018. "Appeals Court Reverses Intake Injunction." *Billings Gazette*, https://billingsgazette.com/news/local/lawsuit-filed-over-fate-of-dinosaur-like-river-fish/article_fded1176-7a0f-5cad-bc44-cd981def5382.html

Jenkins, W. 2016. "Sustainability Theory." In *Berkshire Encyclopedia of Sustainability*, eds. R.C. Anderson, 380–384. Great Barrington, MA: Berkshire Publishing. www.berkshirepublishing.com/assets_news/sustainability/Spirit_SustainabilityTheory.pdf

Johnson, W.C., M.D. Dixon, M.L. Scott, L. Rabbe, G. Larson, M. Volke, and B. Werner. 2012. "Forty Years of Vegetation Change on the Missouri River Floodplain." *BioScience* 62, no. 2, pp. 123–135. https://doi.org/10.1525/bio.2012.62.2.6

Jones, B. Spring 2008. "The Endangered Gray Wolf in Wyoming: Managing Wolf Populations after Endangered Species Act Delisting." *Policy Perspectives* 15, pp. 57–82. https://doi.org/10.4079/pp.v15i1.4153

Jones, D. January 29, 2014. "Avian-Habitat Relationships: A Literature Review and Assessment, Final Report." In *Collaboration With the Yellowstone River Conservation District Council Technical Advisory Committee and Montana Audubon*, http://ftp.geoinfo.msl.mt.gov/Documents/Projects/Yellowstone_River_Clearinghouse/AvianHabitatRelationshipsReportFinal29Jan2014.pdf

Jordan, G.R. March 2013. "Draft Revised Recovery Plan for the Pallid Sturgeon (*Scaphirhynchus Albus*)." Billings, MT: U.S. Fish and Wildlife Service, Northern Rockies Fish and Wildlife Conservation Office. www.fws.gov/mountain-prairie/es/species/fish/pallidSturgeon/DrafRevisedRecoveryPlanMarch2013.pdf

Kajikawa, Y., O. Saito, and K. Takeuchi. 2017. "Academic Landscape of 10 Years of Sustainability Science." *Sustainability Science* 12, no. 6, pp. 869–873. https://doi.org/10.1007/s11625-017-0477-6

Kates, R.W., W.C. Clark, R. Corell, J.M. Hall, C.C. Jaeger, I. Lowe, J.J. McCarthy, et al. 2001. "Sustainability Science." *Science* 292, no. 5517, 641–642. www.doi.org/10.1126/science.1059386

Kellogg, W. 2016. "Yellowstone River Recommended Practices & Position Statements: Practical Applications." Clancy, MT: Stream & Water Consulting. https://ftpgeoinfo.msl.mt.gov/Documents/Projects/Yellowstone_River_Clearinghouse/Yellowstone_River_YRRPs_Final03_01_2016.pdf

Kluz, N. 2021. "Smith River State Park and River Corridor: Visitor Use & Statistics Monitoring Report." *Montana Fish, Wildlife, and Parks, Montana State Parks*. https://fwp.mt.gov/binaries/content/assets/fwp/stateparks/smith-river/smith-river-annual-report---2020.pdf

Knouft, J.H., A. Botero-Acosta, C.L. Wu, B. Charry, M.L. Chu, A.I. Dell, . . . S.J. Herrington. 2021. "Forested Riparian Buffers as Climate Adaptation Tools for Management of Riverine Flow and Thermal Regimes: A Case Study in the Meramec River Basin." *Sustainability* 13, no. 4, p. 1877. https://doi.org/10.3390/su13041877

Knowles, J. December 01, 1868. "Opinion." *Territory of Montana v. Drennan*, 1 Mont. 41.1868. Montana Supreme Court, https://cite.case.law/mont/1/41/

Knox, P.L., and S.A. Marston. 2016. *Human Geography: Places and Regions in Global Context*, 7th ed. Toronto, Canada: Pearson Prentice Hall.

Leber, R. July 26, 2012. "Top Two Oil Companies Earn $160,000 Per Minute, Paid Low Tax Rate." *ThinkProgress*. https://thinkprogress.org/top-two-oil-companies-earn-160-000-per-minute-paid-low-tax-rate-48c32ffb79c/

Legatum Institute. 2019. "The Legatum Prosperity Index: A Tool for Transformation" 13th ed. London, UK: The Legatum Institute Foundation. https://prosperitysite.s3-accelerate.amazonaws.com/8115/8635/0367/The_Legatum_Prosperity_Index_2019.pdf

Lesica, P. 2012. *Manual of Montana Vascular Plants*. Fort Worth, TX: Botanical Research Institute of Texas.

Livingston Depot Foundation. n.d. "About the Depot." Livingston Depot Foundation, Livingston, MT. www.livingstondepot.org/about-the-depot.html (accessed June 26, 2020).

Lower Yellowstone River Coalition. 2021. "Who We Are." About. www.loweryellowstoneriver.com/about (accessed February 05, 2021).

Luthar, S.S. 2006. "Resilience in Development: A Synthesis of Research across Five Decades." In *Developmental Psychopathology: Risk, Disorder, and Adaptation*, eds D. Cicchetti and D.J. Cohen, 740–795. New York, NY: Wiley.

Machado, C.F., and J.P. Davim, eds. 2020. *Sustainable Management for Managers and Engineers*. Hoboken, NJ: John Wiley & Sons, Inc.

Machtinger. E.T. January 2007. "Riparian Systems." *Fish and Wildlife Habitat Management Leaflet, Number*, 45. Helena, MT: Natural Resources and Conservation Service and Wildlife Habitat Council. www.nrcs.usda.gov/Internet/FSE_DOCUMENTS/nrcs143_010137.pdf.

Mahoney, J.M., and S.B. Rood. 1998. "Streamflow Requirements for Cottonwood Seedling Recruitment—An Integrative Model." *Wetlands* 18, no. 4, pp. 634–645. https://doi.org/10.1007/BF03161678

Maître, V., A.C. Cosandey, E. Desagher, and A. Parriaux. 2003. "Effectiveness of Groundwater Nitrate Removal in a River Riparian Area: The Importance of Hydrogeological Conditions." *Journal of Hydrology* 278, no. 1–4, pp. 76–93. https://doi.org/10.1016/S0022-1694(03)00134-3

Mani, V., and C. Delgado. 2019. "Review of Literature." In *Supply Chain Social Sustainability for Manufacturing.* India Studies in Business and Economics, 11–80. Singapore: Springer. https://doi.org/10.1007/978-981-13-1241-0_2

Martin, E. January 09, 2019. *The Government Shutdown Spotlights a Bigger Issue: 78% of US Workers Live Paycheck to Paycheck. CNBC.*

McEvoy, J., S.J. Gilbertz, M.B. Anderson, K.J. Ormerod, and N.T. Bergmann. 2017. "Cultural Theory of Risk as a Heuristic for Understanding Perceptions of Oil and Gas Development in Eastern Montana, USA." *The Extractive Industries and Society* 4, no. 4, pp. 852–859. https://doi.org/10.1016/j.exis.2017.10.004

McKenzie, S. 2004. "Social Sustainability: Towards Some Definitions." *Hawke Research Institute Working Papers Series,* no. 27. Magill, South Australia: University of South Australia. www.unisa.edu.au/siteassets/episerver-6-files/documents/eass/hri/working-papers/wp27.pdf

Merigliano, M.F., J.M. Friedman, and M.L. Scott. 2013. "Tree-Ring Records of Variation in Flow and Channel Geometry." In *Treatise on Geomorphology* 12, Ecogeomorphology, eds. J.F. Shroder (Editor-in-chief), and D.R. Butler and C.R. Hupp (Volume Editors), 145–164. San Diego, CA: Academic Press. https://doi.org/10.1016/B978-0-12-374739-6.00319-5

Miller, K., and T. Quinn. n.d. "Yellowstone River Basin." *Fact Sheet 149–97.* Cheyenne, WY: U.S. Geological Survey, Water Resources Division, National Water-Quality Assessment Program. https://pubs.usgs.gov/fs/FS-149-97/fs-149-97.pdf (accessed June 26, 2020).

Miller, T.R. 2013. "Constructing Sustainability Science: Emerging Perspectives and Research Trajectories." *Sustainability Science* 8, pp. 279–293. https://doi.org/10.1007/s11625-012-0180-6

Montana Board of Oil and Gas Production. 2007. "Horizontal Permit Count." Billings, MT: Montana Department of Natural Resources and Conservation. www.bogc.dnrc.mt.gov/WebApps/DataMiner/Statistics/StatHorzPermitCount.aspx (accessed June 26, 2020).

Montana Code Annotated. 1985. Title 23, Chapter 2, Part 302. https://leg.mt.gov/bills/mca/title_0230/chapter_0020/part_0030/section_0020/0230-0020-0030-0020.html

Montana Department of Environmental Quality. June 02, 2020. *Water Quality Planning and TMDL Project Areas.* Helena, MT: Montana Department of

Environmental Quality, TMDL Development Status, Yellowstone River Basin. http://deq.mt.gov/Water/SurfaceWater/TMDL/tpamap

Montana Department of Justice. September 16, 2016. "Governor, AG Announce $12 Million Settlement." *Montana Department of Justice Press Release.* https://news.mt.gov/governor-steve-bullock-attorney-general-tim-fox-announce-12-million-settlement-for-natural-resource-damage-from-2011-yellowstone-river-oil-spill

Montana Department of Natural Resources and Conservation. n.d. "Marketing Water Rights." Helena, MT: Montana Department of Natural Resources and Conservation. http://dnrc.mt.gov/divisions/water/water-rights/marketing-water-rights (accessed June 30, 2020).

Montana Department of Natural Resources and Conservation. 1995. *Montana Drought Response Plan, 1995.* Helena, MT: Montana Department of Natural Resources and Conservation. http://dnrc.mt.gov/divisions/water/drought-management/montana-drought-management-plan-mdmp-update

Montana Department of Natural Resources and Conservation. 2014. "Yellowstone River Basin Water Plan 2014." Helena, MT: Montana Department of Natural Resources and Conservation and Yellowstone Basin Advisory Council. http://dnrc.mt.gov/divisions/water/management/docs/state-water-plan/yellowstone/river-basin-plan/yellowstone_river_basin_report_final.pdf

Montana Department of Natural Resources and Conservation. April 2015a. "How Are Instream Flows Protected?" Water Fact Sheets #8. Helena, MT: Montana Department of Natural Resources and Conservation and Montana Watercourse, http://dnrc.mt.gov/divisions/water/management/docs/training-and-education/8_how_are_instream_flows_protected.pdf

Montana Department of Natural Resources and Conservation. April 2015b. "How Is Water Managed in the Event of Water Shortages?" Water Fact Sheets #6. Helena, MT: Montana Department of Natural Resources and Conservation and Montana Watercourse. https://static1.squarespace.com/static/5498382ce4b015fce7f847a2/t/57c7244c9f7456b915e34ccf/1472668777218/WaterFactSheets_ALL.pdf

Montana Department of Natural Resources and Conservation. June 2016. "Montana's Basin Closures and Controlled Groundwater Areas." Helena, MT: Water Resources Division, Water Rights Bureau. http://dnrc.mt.gov/divisions/water/water-rights/docs/new-appropriations/montana-basin-closures-and-controlled-groundwater-areas-2016.pdf

Montana Fish, Wildlife and Parks. June 27, 2016a. "Miles City Fish Hatchery Hosts Prehistoric Visitors." *Fishing News Release*, Helena, MT: Montana Fish, Wildlife and Parks, Region 7. www.roundupweb.com/story/2016/07/06/outdoors/miles-city-fish-hatchery-hosts-prehistoric-visitors/8342.html

Montana Fish, Wildlife and Parks. August 19, 2016b. "Yellowstone River Closed in Response to Ongoing Fish Kill." Montana Fish, Wildlife and Parks News Release, www.nps.gov/yell/learn/news/16051.htm

Montana State Library. n.d. "Yellowstone River Clearinghouse." Natural Resource Information System, Montana State Library. https://geoinfo.msl.mt.gov/data/yellowstone_river_corridor_resource_clearinghouse (accessed March 01, 2021).

Montana Trout Unlimited. 2021. "About the Smith." *Smith River Watch*, Missoula, Montana. www.smithriverwatch.org/about-the-smith/floating/.

Morris, C. April 18, 2018. "42% of Americans have Less Than $10,000 Saved for Retirement." *Fortune.*

Murphy, B. 1968. "The Lawyer as Historian: Magna Carta and Public Rights of Fishery." *Irish Jurist*, New Series 3, no. 1, 131–145. www.jstor.org/stable/44026065

Museum of the Yellowstone. n.d. "Travel by Train." West Yellowstone, MT: Yellowstone Historic Center. https://museumoftheyellowstone.org/trains (accessed June 26, 2020).

National Agricultural Statistics Service. 2017. "2017 Census of Agriculture - County Data: Table 45. Selected Operation and Producer Characteristics." U.S. Department of Agriculture, National Agricultural Statistics Service: 528–57. www.nass.usda.gov/Publications/AgCensus/2017/Full_Report/Volume_1,_Chapter_2_County_Level/Montana/st30_2_0045_0045.pdf.

National Research Council. 2011. *Sustainability and the U.S. EPA.* Washington, DC: The National Academies Press. https://doi.org/10.17226/13152

Nielsen, J.L., S.B. Rood, D.W. Pearce, M.G. Letts, H. Jiskoot, and J. Ehleringer. 2010. "Streamside Trees: Responses of Male, Female and Hybrid Cottonwoods to Flooding." *Tree Physiology* 30, no. 12, pp. 1479–1488. https://doi.org/10.1093/treephys/tpq089

Norton, B.G., and A. Thompson. 2014. "Ethics and Sustainable Development: The Virtues of an Adaptive Approach to Environmental Choice." In *Handbook of Sustainable Development*, eds. G. Atkinson, S. Dietz, E. Neumayer, and M. Agarwala, 105–124. Cheltenham, UK: Edward Elgar Publishing.

Our Montana. n.d. "Our Mission." *Our Montana Inc.* Our Mission and History. https://ourmontana.org/about-us/our-mission-and-history/ (accessed January 28, 2021).

Peccia, R. 2013. "Existing and Projected Conditions: Paradise Valley Corridor Planning Study US 89 (Gardiner to Livingston), Final." Helena, MT: Prepared for Montana Department of Transportation by Robert Peccia and Associates, September 16, 2013. www.mdt.mt.gov/pubinvolve/paradisevalley/docs/ep-report.pdf

Peterson, T.R. 1997. *Sharing the Earth: The Rhetoric of Sustainable Development.* Columbia, SC: University of South Carolina Press.

Public Land/Water Access Association. n.d. "Mission Statement." https://plwa.org (accessed January 28, 2021).

Purvis, B., Y. Mao, and D. Robinson. 2019. "Three Pillars of Sustainability: In Search of Conceptual Origins." *Sustainability Science* 14, no. 3, pp. 681–695. https://doi.org/10.1007/s11625-018-0627-5

Randle, T.J. April 02–06, 2006. "Channel Migration Model for Meandering Rivers." Proceedings of the Eighth Federal Interagency Sedimentation Conference, Reno, NV. https://acwi.gov/sos/pubs/8thFISC/Session%204B-2_Randle.pdf.

"Reach Narrative B2." August 20, 2015. Cumulative Effects Analysis, Yellowstone River Reach Narratives, Area B2, 7–10. Co-Sponsored by the Yellowstone River Conservation District Council and the U.S. Army Corps of Engineers. http://ftp.geoinfo.msl.mt.gov/Documents/Projects/Yellowstone_River_Clearinghouse/Yellowstone_Reach_Narratives_2015.pdf

"Reach Narrative B3." 2015. Cumulative Effects Analysis, Yellowstone River Reach Narratives, Area B3, August 20, 2015: 11–14. Co-Sponsored by the Yellowstone River Conservation District Council and the U.S. Army Corps of Engineers. http://ftp.geoinfo.msl.mt.gov/Documents/Projects/Yellowstone_River_Clearinghouse/Yellowstone_Reach_Narratives_2015.pdf

Robbins, P. 2004. *Political Ecology*. Oxford, UK: Blackwell Publishers.

Robbins, P., S. Martin, and S. Gilbertz. 2012. "Developing the Commons: The Contradictions of Growth in Exurban Montana." *Professional Geographer* 64, no. 3, 317–331. https://doi-org/10.1080/00330124.2011.601193

Robison, J. May 29, 2019. "Millennials Worry About the Environment—Should Your Company?" *Gallup*. Workplace. www.gallup.com/workplace/257786/millennials-worry-environment-company.aspx

Røpke, I. 2004. "The Early History of Modern Ecological Economics." *Ecological Economics* 50, nos. 3–4, pp. 293–314. https://doi.org/10.1016/j.ecolecon.2004.02.012

Ross, M., and Bateman, N. January 08, 2020. "Low Unemployment Isn't Worth Much of the Jobs Barely Pay." Brookings Institution.

Sage, J. 2016. "Economic Contributions of the Yellowstone River to Park County." *Institute for Tourism and Recreation Research Publications*, 346. https://scholarworks.umt.edu/itrr_pubs/346

Schaltegger, S., E.G. Hansen, and F. Lüdeke-Freund. 2015. "Business Models for Sustainability: Origins, Present Research, and Future Avenues." *Organization & Environment* 29, no. 1, pp. 3–10. https://doi.org/10.1177/1086026615599806

Scheid, B. October 31, 2018. "Continental Resources Doubles Estimate for Bakken Oil Recovery." *S&P Global Platts*, reported by Meridian Energy Group Inc. www.meridianenergygroupinc.com/continental-resources-doubles-estimate-for-bakken-oil-recovery/

Schneiders, R.K. 1999. *Unruly River: Two Centuries of Change Along the Missouri.* Lawrence, KS: University Press of Kansas.

Schook, D.M., J.M. Friedman, and S.L. Rathburn. 2016. "Flow Reconstructions in the Upper Missouri River Basin Using Riparian Tree Rings." *Water Resources Research* 52, no. 10, pp. 8159–8173. https://doi.org/10.1002/2016WR018845

Schweier, J., N. Magagnotti, E.R. Labelle, and D. Athanassiadis. 2019. "Sustainability Impact Assessment of Forest Operations: A Review." *Current Forestry Reports* 5, no. 2, pp. 101–113. https://doi.org/10.1007/s40725-019-00091-6

Scott, M.L., G.T. Auble, and J.M. Friedman. 1997. "Flood Dependency of Cottonwood Establishment along the Missouri River, Montana, USA." *Ecological Applications* 7, no. 2, pp. 677–690. https://doi.org/10.1890/1051-0761(1997)007[0677:FDOCEA]2.0.CO;2

Serbina, L., and L. Donovan. 2015. "Socioeconomic Report: Regional Profile of the Yellowstone River Corridor." Fort Collins, CO: U.S. Geological Survey, Fort Collins Science Center. http://ftp.geoinfo.msl.mt.gov/Documents/Projects/Yellowstone_River_Clearinghouse/SocioEconomic_2015_Part1.pdf.

Shearman, R. 1990. "The Meaning and Ethics of Sustainability." *Environmental Management* 14, no. 1, pp. 1–8. https://doi.org/10.1007/BF02394014

Soulé, M.E. 1985. "What Is Conservation Biology?" *BioScience* 35, no. 11, pp. 727–734. https://doi.org/10.2307/1310054

Squillace, M. 1988. "The Enduring Vitality of the General Mining Law of 1872." *Environmental Law Reporter* 18, no. 7, ELR10261. https://elr.info/sites/default/files/articles/18.10261.htm

State and Federal Trustees. January, 2017. "Final Programmatic Damage Assessment and Restoration Plan and Final Programmatic Environmental Assessment for the ExxonMobil Pipeline Company July 01, 2011 Yellowstone River Oil Spill." State of Montana and U.S. Department of the Interior, https://media.dojmt.gov/wp-content/uploads/nrdp-yellowstone-restoration.pdf.

Stern, C.V. 2019. "Indian Water Rights Settlements." CRS Report 44148, Version 21. CRS Report Prepared for Members and Committees of Congress. Washington, DC: Congressional Research Service, Updated April 16, 2019. https://fas.org/sgp/crs/misc/R44148.pdf

Stokes, D.E. 1997. *Pasteur's Quadrant: Basic Science and Technological Innovation* Washington, DC: Brookings Institution Press.

Stuart, J. January 20, 2019. "Intake Project Now Held Up in Dispute Over Bid Award." *Glendive Ranger Review.* www.rangerreview.com/content/intake-project-now-held-dispute-over-bid-award

Svensson, G., and B. Wagner. 2015. "Implementing and Managing Economic, Social and Environmental Efforts of Business Sustainability: Propositions for Measurement and Structural Models." *Management of Environmental Quality* 26, no. 2, pp. 195–213. https://doi.org/10.1108/MEQ-09-2013-0099

United Nations. 2004. *World Population in 2300.* New York, NY: United Nations.

Upper Yellowstone Watershed Group. 2016. "Goals." About Us. www.upperyellowstone.org/about

U.S. Army Corps of Engineers and Yellowstone River Conservation District Council. December 2015. "Yellowstone River Cumulative Effects Analysis." Omaha, NE: U.S. Army Corps of Engineers Omaha District. http://ftp.geoinfo.msl.mt.gov/Documents/Projects/Yellowstone_River_Clearinghouse/Yellowstone-River-Cumulative-Effects-Study.pdf

U.S. Bureau of Reclamation. n.d.a. "Lower Yellowstone Project." *Projects & Facilities: Projects.* www.usbr.gov/projects/index.php?id=346 (accessed on October 16, 2018).

U.S. Bureau of Reclamation. n.d.b. "Pick Sloan Missouri Basin Program." Projects and Facilities, Construction. www.usbr.gov/projects/index.php?id=380 (accessed June 26, 2020).

U.S. Bureau of Reclamation. December 05, 2016. "Record of Decision Signed for Lower Yellowstone Fish Passage Project." *News Release Archive*, www.usbr.gov/newsroom/newsroomold/newsrelease/detail.cfm?RecordID=57556

U.S. Bureau of Reclamation. 2018. "Lower Yellowstone Project." Reclamation: Missouri Basin and Arkansas-Rio Grande-Texas Gulf: Montana Area Office, Last updated June 24, 2020. www.usbr.gov/gp/mtao/loweryellowstone/index.html

U.S. Census Bureau. July 01, 2019a. "QuickFacts: Park County, Montana." www.census.gov/quickfacts/parkcountymontana

U.S. Census Bureau. 2019b. "Suburban." Statshttps://suburbanstats.org/ (accessed June 26, 2020).

U.S. Congress. Senate. December 11, 2019. "Montana Water Rights Protection Act." S.3019. 116th Congress, Introduced by Senator Steve Daines. www.congress.gov/bill/116th-congress/senate-bill/3019/text

U.S. Department of Justice. May 12, 2015. "Reserved Water Rights and the Supreme Court." Environment and Natural Resources Division, Federal Reserved Water Rights and State Law Claims. www.justice.gov/enrd/federal-reserved-water-rights-and-state-law-claims

U.S. Environmental Protection Agency. n.d.a. "Nonpoint Source: Agriculture." Environmental Topics, Polluted Runoff, Nonpoint Source (NPS) Pollution. www.epa.gov/nps/nonpoint-source-agriculture (accessed June 30, 2020).

U.S. Environmental Protection Agency. n.d.b. "Potential Well Water Contaminants and Their Impacts." *Private Wells*, Quick Reference Table. www.epa.gov/privatewells/potential-well-water-contaminants-and-their-impacts (accessed June 30, 2020).

U.S. Environmental Protection Agency. February 04, 2019. "Sources and Solutions." *Nutrient Pollution.* www.epa.gov/nutrientpollution/sources-and-solutions.

U.S. Environmental Protection Agency. June 11, 2020. "Environmental Justice." www.epa.gov/environmentaljustice

U.S. Fish and Wildlife Service. June 15, 2020. "About Garrison Dam National Fish Hatchery." Riverdale, ND: U.S. Fish and Wildlife Service, Mountain-Prairie Region, Garrison Dam National Fish Hatchery, www.fws.gov/mountain-prairie/fisheries/garrisonDam.php

U.S. Geological Survey. n.d.a. "How Much Oil and Gas are Actually in the Bakken Formation?" *Energy*, www.usgs.gov/faqs/how-much-oil-and-gas-are-actually-bakken-formation?qt-news_science_products=0#qt-news_science_products (accessed June 26, 2020).

U.S. Geological Survey. n.d.b. "How Much Water Does the Typical Hydraulically Fractured Well Require?" *Energy*, www.usgs.gov/faqs/how-much-water-does-typical-hydraulically-fractured-well-require?qt-news_science_products=0#qt-news_science_products (accessed June 26, 2020).

U.S. Geological Survey. n.d.c "Yellowstone River Compact Commission." *Water Resources*, www.usgs.gov/mission-areas/water-resources/science/yellowstone-river-compact-commission?qt-science_center_objects=0#qt-science_center_objects (accessed February 12, 2021).

U.S. Geological Survey. 2005. "Changes in Streamflow Timing in the Western United States in Recent Decades." Fact Sheet no. 2005-3018. La Jolla, CA: U.S. Geological Survey, March 2005. https://pubs.usgs.gov/fs/2005/3018/

U.S. Geological Survey. 2013. "Assessment of Undiscovered Oil Resources in the Bakken and Three Forks Formations, Williston Basin Province, Montana, North Dakota, and South Dakota." National Assessment of Oil and Gas Fact Sheet no. 2013-3013. U.S. Geological Survey, Bakken-Three Forks Assessment Team. https://pubs.usgs.gov/fs/2013/3013/fs2013-3013.pdf

U.S. National Park Service. 2015 "Yellowtail Dam." Big Horn Canyon. Lovell, WY: U.S. Department of the Interior, National Park Service. Last updated February 2, 2015. www.nps.gov/bica/learn/historyculture/yellowtail-dam.htm

Van de Lande, L. 2015. "Eliminating Discrimination and Inequalities in Access to Water and Sanitation." Geneva, Switzerland: United Nations Water Technical Advisory Unit. www.unwater.org/publications/eliminating-discrimination-inequalities-access-water-sanitation/

Vidon, P.G., M.K. Welsh, and Y.T. Hassanzadeh. 2019. "Twenty Years of Riparian Zone Research (1997–2017): Where to Next?" *Journal of Environmental Quality* 48, no. 2, pp. 248–260. https://doi.org/10.2134/jeq2018.01.0009

Ward, L., M.B. Anderson, S.J. Gilbertz, J. McEvoy, and D.M. Hall. July 2017. "Public Stealth and Boundary Objects: Coping with Integrated Water Resource Management and the Post-Political Condition in Montana's Portion of the Yellowstone River Watershed." *Geoforum* 83, pp. 1–13. https://doi.org/10.1016/j.geoforum.2017.04.017

Water Policy Interim Committee. 2018. "Water Rights in Montana." Helena, MT: Montana Department of Natural Resources and Conservation, Water Bureau Division, February 2018. https://leg.mt.gov/content/Publications/Environmental/2018-water-rights-handbook-final.pdf

Wiek, A., B. Ness, P. Schweizer-Ries, F.S. Brand, and F. Farioli. 2012. "From Complex Systems Analysis to Transformational Change: A Comparative Appraisal of Sustainability Science Projects." *Sustainability Science* 7, no. S1, pp. 5–24. https://doi.org/10.1007/s11625-011-0148-y

World Bank. 2006. *The Road to 2050*. Washington DC: World Bank.

Worster, D.E. 1994. *Nature's Economy: A History of Ecological Ideas*, 2nd ed. Cambridge, UK: Cambridge University Press.

Yellowstone National Parks Trips. January 21, 2007. "Yellowstone Lake by the Numbers." *Natural Wonders Series*. www.yellowstonepark.com/things-to-do/yellowstone-lake-numbers

Yellowstone River Conservation Districts Council. n.d.a. "Current Projects." https://yellowstonerivercouncil.org/current-projects/ (accessed February 16, 2021).

Yellowstone River Conservation Districts Council. n.d.b. "Interactive Map of the Yellowstone River." Helena, MT: Montana State Library. http://montana.maps.arcgis.com/apps/webappviewer/index.html?id=3fc5b219f4494ebab2477e93a5bbecca (accessed June 30, 2020).

Zentz, J.I. 2001. "Montana Agriculture: The Evolution of an Aging Industry." Graduate Student Theses, Dissertations, & Professional Papers. 3002. Master of Arts thesis, University of Montana. https://scholarworks.umt.edu/etd/3002

About the Authors

Susan J. Gilbertz, PhD is a professor of Geography and acting associate dean of the College of Business at Montana State University Billings. She grew up on a cattle ranch in rural Wyoming, and she earned BS and MA degrees in Communication from the University of Wyoming. Her PhD from Texas A&M University prepared her to return to the high plains, where she has focused on how senses of place influence environmental values and willingness to share natural resources. She has studied the people and resources of the Yellowstone River for over 17 years, and she has overseen more than 500 interviews with the people of the valley. Her projects have been sponsored by the U.S. Army Corps of Engineers, the National Science Foundation, the National Institutes of Health, the Montana Department of Natural Resources and Conservation, the Yellowstone River Conservation District Council, the Harry L. Willett Foundation, and Montana State University Billings. Her publications can be found in the *Annals of the American Association of Geographers*, *Geoforum*, *Professional Geographer*, *Land Use Policy*, *Water Resources Management*, *Journal of Environmental Studies and Sciences*, *Journal of Environmental Policy & Planning*, *Environmental Politics*, *European Journal of Sustainable Development*, and the *Council on Undergraduate Research Quarterly*, to name a few.

Damon M. Hall, PhD is an assistant professor at the University of Missouri in the School of Natural Resources and jointly appointed in Biomedical, Biological and Chemical Engineering. He received his BS in Agriculture and MA in Communication from Purdue University. He completed a PhD in Wildlife and Fisheries Sciences at Texas A&M University as a Boone and Crockett Conservation Policy Fellow. His dissertation, *Managing the Yellowstone River System with Place-Based Cultural Data*, is an analysis of the 2006 Yellowstone Cultural Inventory data. After a postdoctoral fellowship in sustainability science at the University of Maine's Sustainability Solutions Initiative, he was an assistant professor in the Center for Sustainability and Department of Biology at Saint Louis University prior to joining the University of Missouri. In 2018, Damon joined the College of Engineering's Sustainability in FEWSed (Food, Energy, Water, Smart Cities) research pillar. He is codirector of the Missouri Water Center, certificate coordinator for the undergraduate Certificate in Sustainability, and an affiliated faculty member in the Harry S. Truman School of Public Affairs. Dr. Hall's research examines the human dimensions of sustainability challenges where science, policy, and culture meet. At Mizzou, he heads the Sustainability Science Lab (SustainabilityScienceLab.org), which includes projects in water resources planning, insect pollinator conservation, and communicating social–ecological systems models. His research has been sponsored by the National Science Foundation, U.S. Army Corps of Engineers, U.S. Department of Agriculture, National Park Service, and the Missouri Departments of Conservation and Natural Resources. His publications can be found in *Conservation Biology*, *Sustainability Science*, *Environmental Science & Policy*, *Journal of Environmental Management*, *Journal of Cleaner Production*, *Environmental Modelling & Software*, *Water Resources Management*, and *Water Resources Research*, to name a few.

Index

CPSIA information can be obtained
at www.ICGtesting.com
Printed in the USA
JSHW050146090822
29051JS00008B/265

9 781637 421475